THIS TIME I WILL Praise THE LORD

This Time I Will Praise the Lord is a refreshingly authentic journey into the heart of praise. With honesty, compassion, and biblical insight, Darren reminds us that praise isn't about perfect circumstances, but about trusting the perfect character of God. This book will inspire you to lift your eyes above your pain and challenges to declare, like Leah, "This time I will praise the Lord!" A must-read for anyone longing to experience God's goodness in every season of life.

—Susan Elsmore
Associate Pastor, Mackenzie Campus, Gateway Baptist Church

I first met Darren around ten years ago and was struck by his authentic love for God, his grace and genuineness towards people. This book unpacks those same values that he lives out. It offers a biblical perspective towards God's praise, grace, and strength no matter what season of life you are in, and the path to action it. I definitely recommend this read.

—Michael W. Smith
Association of Related Churches (ARC), COO

Praise God for this book! For the last twenty years, I have seen Darren choose to praise God on the mountaintop and in the valley. This book is not just theory but a beautiful and biblical reflection of the power of praise in every season of life. If you love God and you want to learn to express your love for Him even more, you will love this book.

—Jason Elsmore
Senior Pastor, Gateway Baptist Church
Director of the Queensland Baptist Movement

A resounding praise comes from my heart as I finish reading Darren's book about giving God all of our praise, no matter where life's journey takes us. Darren speaks from his own lived experience and brings fresh insights from God's Word, especially as he unwraps the heart-wrenching story of Leah. He offers practical ideas to encourage and teach us to praise, listen, and trust God daily.

—Melanie Easton
Christian Book & Music, Co-owner

Darren explains how the trials and disappointments of Jacob's wife Leah can teach us profound lessons if we learn to praise God in the midst of our own struggles. His intent is to encourage readers to approach life's journey counterculturally.

—Sal Biondolillo
Pioneering Company Chaplain, Lynden Door Inc.

Darren writes in a way that reflects the man I know and have considered a good friend for over four decades. He is theologically thoughtful and deeply pastoral. More than a great encouragement as to the purpose and power of praise, this book invites us to something greater—the transformative power of learning to apply it to your own life no matter what season you are in. The words will encourage and its godly application can transform.

—Andrew Mayne
Lead Campus Pastor, Gateway Baptist Church

THIS TIME I WILL Praise THE LORD

How Leah's Passionate Declaration Helped Shape History

DARREN ABRAHAMS

THIS TIME I WILL PRAISE THE LORD
Copyright © 2025 by Darren Abrahams

All rights reserved. Neither this publication nor any part of this publication may be reproduced or transmitted in any form or by any means, electronic or mechanical, including photocopying, recording or any information storage and retrieval system, without permission in writing from the author.

Unless otherwise indicated, scripture quotations taken from The Holy Bible, New International Version®, NIV®. Copyright © 1973, 1978, 1984, 2011 by Biblica, Inc. Used with permission of Zondervan. All rights reserved worldwide. www.zondervan.com Scripture quotations marked (NLT) are taken from the Holy Bible, New Living Translation, copyright ©1996, 2004, 2015 by Tyndale House Foundation. Used by permission of Tyndale House Publishers, Carol Stream, Illinois 60188. All rights reserved. Scripture quotations marked MSG are taken from The Message, copyright © 1993, 2002, 2018 by Eugene H. Peterson. Used by permission of NavPress. All rights reserved. Represented by Tyndale House Publishers. Scripture quotations are from the ESV® Bible (The Holy Bible, English Standard Version®), © 2001 by Crossway, a publishing ministry of Good News Publishers. ESV Text Edition: 2025. The ESV text may not be quoted in any publication made available to the public by a Creative Commons license. The ESV may not be translated in whole or in part into any other language. Used by permission. All rights reserved. Scripture quotations marked (CEV) are from the Contemporary English Version Copyright © 1991, 1992, 1995 by American Bible Society. Used by Permission. Scripture quotations taken from the Amplified® Bible (AMP), Copyright © 2015 by The Lockman Foundation. Used by permission. lockman.org Scripture quotations taken from the (NASB®) New American Standard Bible®, Copyright © 1960, 1971, 1977, 1995, 2020 by The Lockman Foundation. Used by permission. All rights reserved. lockman.org Scripture quotations marked CSB have been taken from the Christian Standard Bible®, Copyright © 2017 by Holman Bible Publishers. Used by permission. Christian Standard Bible® and CSB® are federally registered trademarks of Holman Bible Publishers. Scripture quotations marked GNT taken from the Good News Translation® (Today's English Version, Second Edition) © 1992 American Bible Society. All rights reserved. All Scripture marked with the designation "GW" is taken from GOD'S WORD®. © 1995, 2003, 2013, 2014, 2019, 2020 by God's Word to the Nations Mission Society. Used by permission. Scripture quoted by permission. Quotations designated (NET) are from the NET Bible® copyright ©1996, 2019 by Biblical Studies Press, L.L.C. https://netbible.com All rights reserved. Scripture quotations marked BSB taken from the Berean Standard Bible, which is in the public domain. Scripture taken from the Holy Bible: International Standard Version® Release 2.0. Copyright © 1996-2013 by the ISV Foundation. Used by permission of Davidson Press, LLC. ALL RIGHTS RESERVED INTERNATIONALLY. Scripture quotations marked TPT are from The Passion Translation®. Copyright © 2017, 2018, 2020 by Passion & Fire Ministries, Inc. Used by permission. All rights reserved. ThePassionTranslation.com. Scripture quotations marked DRB taken from the Douay-Rheims Bible, which is in the public domain.

ISBN: 978-1-4866-2742-4
eBook ISBN: 978-1-4866-2743-1

Word Alive Press
119 De Baets Street Winnipeg, MB R2J 3R9
www.wordalivepress.ca

Cataloguing in Publication information can be obtained from Library and Archives Canada.

This book is dedicated to my loving heavenly Father and Saviour Jesus, the ultimate source of my praise. I am forever thankful for everything You have blessed me with, including Kristy, Sierra, and Cody, my extended family, my covenant friends, and all who helped focus me on the eternal praise due Your name.

CONTENTS

ACKNOWLEDGEMENTS   xi
FOREWORD   xiii

Introduction
CHOICES   xv

1: *The Backstory*   1

2: *Leah's First Son, Reuben*
(BECAUSE #1)   13

3: *Leah's Second Son, Simeon*
(BECAUSE #2)   27

4: *Leah's Third Son, Levi*
(BECAUSE #3)   45

5: *Leah's Fourth Son, Judah*   59

6: *Praise Has Bad Days,*
BUT PRAISE SEES THE END   77

7: *Judah's Unfolding Story*   91

8: *A Divine Genealogy*   107

Conclusion
   LAUS DEO   121

ABOUT THE AUTHOR   129
BIBLIOGRAPHY   131

ACKNOWLEDGEMENTS

Unsurprisingly, any feat such as this is a team effort, and I am extremely grateful to stand as one of many who made this book a reality. I am thankful for the Holy Spirit's inspiration for this concept and the incredible encouragement of my wife Kristy, Mum, Dad, sister Kylie, and brother Peter. Furthermore, I am deeply appreciative of the insights and assistance of numerous pastors, friends, and colleagues, including the Word Alive Press team who have mentored me along this journey in giving clear voice towards the goal of godly praise.

FOREWORD

Rejected. Pain. Overlooked. Refused. Have you ever felt the depth and weight of those words when it comes to your life? Chances are we all have. I know I have. These words affect our hearts, plague our minds, and leave us confused and wounded.

Unfortunately, our current societal structures reflect the behaviours of cancel culture and social exclusion, which have instilled fear and isolation in so many. Where do we turn, given these honest admissions? What do we do when these real-life experiences occur? Humanity needs a catalytic change to adjust such detrimental patterns.

I believe my friend Darren provides an antidote. His book, *This Time I Will Praise the Lord*, is a very timely resource. Through his own personal life experiences and professional journey of being a pastor, counsellor, and chaplain, his transparency and wisdom provide an answer for those willing to engage.

In my thirty years of being a pastor, I have never been handed a book about the life of a Hebrew woman named Leah, whose story is found in the biblical account of Genesis 29. Yes, I have heard messages spoken about her, as well as illustrations that I have applied to my own life. But please notice: one of the first identifiers about Leah is that she had lazy eyes, or weak eyes, and is one whom society overlooked. That's not a favourable introduction at all and led to much pain and rejection.

Leah's story goes much deeper than her eyes. It is riddled with negative comparisons, continuous competition, pervasive anxiety, and feelings of being unloved. You and I can relate to Leah in some capacity, though maybe not in the lazy eyes department.

Despite incredible pain and rejection, a tangible shift happens in her heart. Her life is divinely transformed and echoes one statement that should compel us all to carefully consider our next step: 'This time I will praise the Lord." This isn't praise towards herself or someone else or in a circumstance, but rather praise of the Lord. The invitation is to take our eyes off the situation and place them on the One who will always help us.

The negative mindsets within us begin to shift when praise is practiced and lived out. Let me invite you on a journey to explore and experience what praise can do. Be encouraged and strengthened through Darren's words; they will leave you in a better place. I'm speaking from my personal experience with him!

But may I please advocate for this one thing from you? Make sure your praise is directed to Jesus and to Him alone. That way, the purpose of this book will be fulfilled. Let's praise!

—Shawn Chapman
Lead Pastor, Colwood Church, Canada

Introduction

CHOICES

...whenever we praise God best, we simply declare what he is, for the bare fact about God is the highest praise... the grateful mention of his glorious acts is in itself adoration.[1]
—Charles Spurgeon

Friend, in this moment we have a choice. Obviously we make a thousand life choices every day about many different things. For example, what time will I set my alarm? Will I go to the gym or hit the snooze button? What will I wear? Some decisions are less important while others carry significant weight, like should I maintain my integrity when I'm falsely accused? What career should I pursue? Which action do I pursue if my marriage fails or my kids act out?

We struggle under anxiety's weighty burden, hoping that life will work out. Alternatively, we can choose to do something radical by pausing and looking heavenward. We can choose to shift our minds from the world's frenetic roar to the Author, Sustainer, and Perfector of life itself. The Lord of heaven and earth longs for us to know Him intentionally

---

[1] Charles Haddon Spurgeon, "The Recorders," *The Spurgeon Center*. June 25, 1876 (https://www.spurgeon.org/resource-library/sermons/the-recorders/#flipbook/).

and intimately while choosing to live a life of praise for the power of His presence.

Genesis 29:35 tells us, *"This time I will praise the Lord."* It's such a simple phrase that one might just pass it by, but it made me stop and pay close attention. It was spoken by our protagonist, Leah, a woman who carried so much pain, hurt, and bitterness, yet she paused and drew a metaphorical line in her painful circumstances.

Leah's choice to praise the Lord catalyzed a heart and mind shift that altered her trajectory so her story could echo with a resonance that still impacts us today. Though this decision didn't come without its challenges, a multitude of events and emotions tried to subvert her resolve. We will explore them as we journey with Leah through the chapters ahead.

Over the past five years, praise has been a valuable teacher for me. But with full disclosure, I took a break from writing this book as my life became heavy and my own praise fell silent. During this pause, I retreated alone to one of my favourite places for reflection. Life had become so burdensome that tears were my only offering.

At one point, I stopped and looked up, dazzled by the sunlight now piercing the grey skies ahead while a vivid rainbow hung steadfast, reminding me of God's promised faithfulness. Please hear me when I write that praise in every season is an ongoing invitation and challenge. God is forever on the throne in good times, hard times, and everything in between; however, our consistent determination to engage this opportunity becomes a praise offering to the Lord who is worthy of all glory and honour.

Our choice to praise God for who He is in every season often generates conflicting emotions. Yet we are called to praise when things don't go the way we want, to trust God's sovereignty even when hope seems lightyears away.

We are exhorted in 2 Corinthians 5:7 to *"walk by faith, not by sight"* (ESV). This seems easy from a heavenly vantage point, but it requires more spiritual muscle for one who's navigating storms here on the earth.

Where do our eyes turn during such seasons? Do we make judgments about God's character based on what we see coming from His hand? Do we allow our emotions to override the truth about His unchanging nature or project our failings onto God's resolute faithfulness and conclude that He falters just like we do?

Our spiritual enemy constantly whispers doubt to help him succeed in his destructive intent towards us. Satan's strategy is to make God's children question His trustworthiness and trust anything but He who is forever faithful. Without careful attention, our enemy dupes us into believing that God is either withholding what is good or failing to protect us from harm.

God's instruction manual is abundantly clear that we should always guard against the enemy's schemes. If we don't make praise an intentional choice, as Leah did, we will be fooled into believing falsity. Romans 1:25 summarizes this faith erosion and abandonment of praise: *"They traded the truth about God for a lie. So they worshiped and served the things God created instead of the Creator himself, who is worthy of eternal praise! Amen"* (NLT).

A practical way to deepen our relationship with the ultimate lover of our souls is through the unfathomable power of praise. Praise focuses our attention on the greatness of God's flawless character. If we choose to make Him greater in our own understanding, His sovereignty is magnified, our perspective is elevated, and Satan loses ground in executing within us his paralyzing anxiety.

MORE THAN A SONG

While living this out experientially, I had a fun conversation with a worship pastor in which I asked for his definition of praise. With a wink and a smile, he said, "The standard for worship music was a slow beat, below 120 beats per minute, while praise was everything faster and required a tambourine. Praise was about singularly giving honour back to the One."

Praise is our intentional choice to rehearse God's perfect goodness amid our circumstances. This often necessitates a perspective shift in our hearts to see a situation through His eyes. Praise is the act of complimenting God for who He is and celebrating His perfection, attributes, virtues, power, authority, wisdom, worthiness, benefits, and excellence.

When pausing to meditate on God's many names, it's easy to become lost in awe and wonder over His majesty and the unfathomable privilege of being adopted as His children. What comes to mind when you celebrate our God as Jehovah Elohim (the Almighty Lord of Creation), Jehovah Adonai (the Lord of Lords), Jehovah Jireh (the Lord will Provide), Jehovah Rophe (the Lord our Healer), Jehovah Shalom (the Lord our Peace), Jehovah Rohi (the Lord my Shepherd), and Jehovah Elohay (the Lord my God), and Yahweh Tsuri (the Lord our Rock)? It's impossible to grasp the magnitude of our Abba Father.

Dr. Roger Barrier, a retired teaching pastor from Tucson, Arizona, outlines eight Hebrew words for praise and how they integrate into our practice. *Hallah* is synonymous with boasting or bragging about God, like how enthusiastic supporters chant at a football match (Psalm 63:3–4). *Yadah* means praising with extended hands in adoration, or crying out for help (Psalm 134:2). *Barak* denotes the transcendent privilege of blessing the Lord for who He is. (Psalm 72:15). *Tehillah* refers to celebrating God with music and singing while celebrating that God Himself is our praise-filled song (Psalm 22:3). *Zamar* speaks to a joyful expression of God's greatness with every available instrument (Psalm 18:1–3). *Todah* and *shabach* both mean loudly praising God with gratitude for His promised deliverance even from within the storm (Psalm 56:1–12).

Hallelujah is the most common expression of praise and transcends all global languages; it's the combination of *hallel* (to boast about) and *jah* (a shortened form of God's name). It's an all-encompassing exuberant exultation to our Lord and Creator. The word is featured in Psalm 150 and used four times in Revelation where the countless multitude of heaven loudly exclaims together, *"Hallelujah! Salvation and glory and power belong to our God"* (Revelation 19:1).

Two other words which are interrelated yet mistakenly substituted for praise are *worship* and *thanksgiving*. These actions are both necessary in our faith journey, but their meanings are important to differentiate. While praise is unidirectional with God's creation, honouring the Creator without requiring a response, worship is relational. Worship involves our connection with God and His reciprocal communion with us. This divine communication flows both ways as we approach God and He graciously bends down to us.

Thanksgiving is rooted in gratitude, celebrating God's goodness for us both individually and corporately. It's about celebrating God for His specific gifts and blessings. For example, we thank God for what He has done in sending His Son Jesus to die for us as a perfect sin offering, as described in John 3:16—*"For God so loved the world, that he gave his only Son, that whoever believes in him should not perish but have everlasting life"* (ESV)—and for the countless benefits He provides for us, including family, friends, housing, clothes, food, employment, finances, and spiritual gifts.

To contrast, our praise doesn't originate from personal gratitude for what He has done but more so from the Holy Spirit's revelation of who God is. When Leah made her seismic declaration that she would praise the Lord, her awesome Father God was the singular target of her devotion. She wasn't just thanking Him for something He had done but choosing to elevate Him above her own bleak circumstances.

In our selfie-driven society, we often need reminders that life isn't simply about us. A phrase my wife and I seek to apply in our family is "think bigger than yourself." Self-centredness invites the subtle allure to satisfy our own desires over those of others, including God, magnifying us as objects of praise. Ultimately, He alone is worthy of all our praise, no matter the season.

Praise, at its heart, was never created to fit the frame of humans. It was designed as a transcendent vehicle for us to magnify the form of God. The psalmist beckons us: *"Praise him for his mighty works; praise his unequaled greatness!"* (Psalm 150:2, NLT) This, my friends, is what I encourage us to do individually and collectively in journeying alongside Leah.

A Willful Act

The Bible is filled with examples of people who are invited to praise God despite what they're experiencing. In 2 Chronicles 20, King Jehoshaphat faced a formidable foreign army that sought to decimate Israel. Despite the alarm bells sounding in his ears, a man named Jahaziel stood up in front of the whole Judean assembly and praised God's sovereignty over the impending battle, exhorting everyone towards a courageous trust in God's ability.

Jehoshaphat then had a choice. As king, he could have cowered in fear and said, "Every man and woman for themselves!" But he chose a different posture. He commissioned a choir to march and sing God's praises ahead of the army as it approached the battlefield. That probably wasn't a common strategy for a military unit, either past or present, but the effect was undeniable: the Lord confused the collaboration of the invading armies, causing them to kill each other until every last opponent was dead. When the tribe of Judah arrived on the scene, they stepped onto a battlefield littered with enemy corpses.

The Bible notes that though fear drove Jehoshaphat to seek God's direction, it was praise that paved the way for God's miracle-working power to stand unchallenged according to His sovereign plan.

When we pause to look heavenward and offer a sacrifice of praise, we leave ourselves little mental real estate for a negative mindset. God will indeed transform our prison of pain into a prism of praise that magnifies His gloriousness.

What an incredible God we serve! Jehovah's unfailing goodness is for every generation, so let's join with all creation in honouring the Lord, our King of heaven and earth.

Praising the Lion

I would suggest that there is no personality in the Bible who always praised God with a smile and a song. Sometimes I chose not to praise because the heartbreak felt devastating. Other times I praised God with tears and heaving sobs. I made the choice to elevate God's character while pain coursed through my body. I have chosen praise during seasons of silence when my heart was so heavy that simply uttering words was a challenge.

My testimony won't reflect your own lived experience, but that's the beauty of them: they offer a window through which to view and celebrate God. For you, praise actions might include journalling, producing simple artwork, taking a silent forest walk, or humbly extending your arms in surrender. Praise invites our whole being—body, soul, and spirit—to align with what we know to be true of our loving heavenly Father through the revelation of the Holy Spirit.

As we'll experience together, praise isn't always pretty or articulate but rather authentic and deliberate. It will be challenged by circumstance, impeded by doubt, and contested by cultural noise. Ultimately, praise is personified in the person of Jesus, who sits triumphantly on heaven's throne at God's right hand; He is the Lion of Judah, encircled and celebrated by the growing population of heaven. Jesus has become the embodiment of praise to our Father God and the Holy Spirit enlivens us to present our offering to the One who is deserving of it all.

Why not join me in asking that the focus of our praise be honoured and elevated as we learn together?

> Loving heavenly Father, Jesus Christ our Saviour, and Holy Spirit our friend, we praise You with everything that is within us. We praise You for Your unending love, Your grace that knows no bounds, Your perfect justice, and Your power that reigns supreme above every power and authority. You are forever with us and leading us towards Your heart of love. We praise You for who You are and for Your perfect purpose, which is forever at work in lives drawing all people towards Your heart. We set our eyes on You and declare, together with Leah, "This time we will praise you, Lord." For Yours is the kingdom, the power, and the glory, both now and forever, amen.

Reflection Time

- In her 2004 song "Indescribable," Laura Story wrestles to describe the greatness of our God. While nothing can ever fully articulate God's greatness, I'm asking that you take time to praise Him while listening to this song and reading the lyrics on YouTube.[2]

---

[2] "Indescribable by Laura Story & Jesse Reeves," *YouTube*. Date of access: August 5, 2025 (https://www.youtube.com/watch?v=UgJFTaKKxkc&list=RDUgJFTaKKxkc&ab_channel=KateSimmonds).

1

The Backstory

When God changes your name, he brings you into his healing power and holy plans. He changes your entire story.[3]

Ever read about the backstory of a movie in tandem with watching it? The context provides a helpful understanding and insight into the artist's process. The same is true in Genesis 29 as Leah waits in the wings for her first appearance. Meanwhile, the curtain rises on the patriarchs and matriarchs who preceded her.

Abraham, Isaac, and Jacob are arguably among the most significant characters in the Old Testament—not because they were men, but because of what God promised and performed through them. The ongoing effects of this promise still impact us today.

Abram, as he was originally known, first appeared in Genesis 11 as the oldest son of his father Terah. Genesis 12 then records Abram hearing from God, with whom he'd had no previous relationship and likely didn't even know. The Bible doesn't say whether the message was audible or a strong mental impression; either way, this interaction profoundly changed

---

[3] "Known by God: God Names Us Forward," *NavPress*. Date of access: July 28, 2025 (https://www.navpress.com/stories/god-names-us-forward).

this man and launched him on a dynamic journey. He was given this divine instruction: *"Leave your native country, your relatives, and your father's family, and go to the land I will show you"* (Genesis 12:1, NLT).

What would you do with a command like that? Being told to leave everything you'd known and go to a foreign country following an unfamiliar deity?

But wait! The command came complete with an incredible multigenerational promise from the Lord:

> I will make you into a great nation. I will bless you and make you famous, and you will be a blessing to others. I will bless those who bless you and curse those who treat you with contempt. All the families on earth will be blessed through you. (Genesis 12:2–3, NLT)

Imagine waking up from a restless night of slumber when you're suddenly interrupted by a divine message that promises to create a great nation through you! Abram may have needed an extra shot of unpasteurized goat's milk in his coffee that day.

The promise he received directly confronted the harsh reality of his present circumstances, given the heartbreak was recorded just three verses earlier: *"But Sarai was unable to become pregnant and had no children"* (Genesis 11:30, NLT).

Naturally speaking, it's ludicrous to even consider how one would start a family, let alone become the father of a "great nation" when your spouse is infertile and IVF was several millennia from even being imagined.

On the flip side, isn't that just like our awesome God to speak His hope-filled promise into our fragile human limitations with the language of His sovereignty?

One trait I admire about Abram was his remarkable obedience. As crazy as the command sounded, he packed up his wife—his whole life, in fact—and followed. No doubt a myriad of thoughts spun through his mind. But whatever his concerns, he resolved to obediently follow God's invitation.

As an evolution of praise begins to mark Abram's faith-filled journey, Yahweh Yireh (the Lord will Provide) changes his name to Abraham, heralding the birth of the couple's miraculous son Isaac.

Paul, a pivotal New Testament apostolic writer, addressed this couple's issue of barrenness: *"Against all hope, Abraham in hope believed and so became the father of many nations, just as it had been said to him, 'So shall your offspring be'"* (Romans 4:18). And it was God for the win yet again. Twenty-five years after God had promised Abraham a nation, his son Isaac became the tangible manifestation of that reality.

Over time, Isaac married Rebekah, who birthed the third link in God's generational plan, a son named Jacob.

All these millennia later, you and I are also the tangible representation of His faithful promise given to those three men. Yes, our God is forever faithful in keeping His promised word to countless generations. So let's start the praise right here!

What's in a Name?

As a father of twin adults, I know that one of the hardest jobs we faced before the birth was choosing their names. Kristy and I sat on the couch for hours trying to decide on the perfect fit for our soon-to-be little munchkins, whom we loved immensely before we ever met them. I had always wanted to choose a biblical name for our son, like Noah or Jonah, but Kristy correctly noted that when added to my surname, it would make the poor kid sound ancient.

Parents might choose to name their children after a family lineage or popular trend. Sometimes these names reflect what we hope our children will become or an admirable character trait we trust they will later embody.

Kristy and I didn't consider any of these scenarios in naming our daughter Sierra, derived from the sawtooth mountain range, and our son Cody, with the Irish root meaning of "little pillow." Honestly, we just liked the sound of these names.

In the Bible, names were often chosen to reflect the circumstances surrounding a child's birth. A few times in Scripture, however, a person's name was divinely changed as their origin no longer matched the result of a godly transformation. For example, Abram's birthname literally meant "exalted father," but fast-forward a few chapters and God renamed him Abraham, meaning "father of a multitude," given the future manifestation of God's faithful promise (Genesis 17:5–6).

When twin brothers Jacob and Esau, Abraham's grandsons, were born to Isaac and Rebekah, the boys emerged with Jacob literally holding onto his older brother's foot. Why? No idea! Maybe he had lost the internal WrestleMania match and had to settle for second place on the podium. So Jacob's name translated to "he grasps the heel" but figuratively meant "he deceives."

This characteristic defined Jacob perfectly. As a young adult, following a hunting expedition, Jacob (the homebody) coerced Esau (the hunter-gatherer) into trading his birthright (future inheritance) for a bowl of stew (Genesis 25:29–34). Furthermore, Jacob deceived his father into bequeathing him God's unique blessing, the one specifically reserved for the firstborn son (Genesis 27:1–30).

Given these deceptions, Esau despised Jacob, and in his emotional volatility he hatched a plan to murder his brother after Isaac died. Rebekah heard about this plan and warned Jacob to flee to her brother's house in a faraway country until Esau's anger could abate.

The storyline makes for compelling reading. The deceiver left in a blaze of dust to find refuge with his uncle Laban, who ironically emerged as a bona fide charlatan himself, as we will soon see.

After arriving in Paddan Aram, Jacob was immediately smitten by an incredibly attractive young lady named Rachel. Stunned by this vision of feminine beauty, Jacob learned that she was Laban's younger daughter. Arrangements were made for Jacob to live with them, as Laban sensed an opportunity to cash in on this potential courtship.

Enter Leah, stage left, but sadly devoid of the same physical allure. Ever heard the story of the ugly duckling? Well, meet our protagonist. The Bible is remarkable at emphasizing small details that add layers of meaning. In comparing the sisters, the Bible says that *"Leah had weak eyes, but Rachel had a lovely figure and was beautiful"* (Genesis 29:17). Other translations expand on these adjectives. One says that Leah's eyes had no sparkle and were ordinary. Another even suggests that she was cross-eyed. The implications of her name have also led some to describe her as being "weary" or "faint from sickness," suggesting that she may have had a congenital birth defect that left her devoid of Rachel's elegance.

So there are no prizes for correctly guessing who Jacob was physically attracted to.

Given his overt love for Rachel, he negotiated a dowry with Laban, exchanging seven years of hard labour for this vision as his wife. You can hear the violins play as the Bible describes the passing of this septennial period; it felt *"like only a few days to him because of his love for her"* (Genesis 29:20, AMP). Aww!

A Marriage of Three

There was an important cultural custom that Laban conveniently forgot to tell Jacob about: families married off their daughters in birth order. The big problem, however, was that nobody wanted Leah. Imagine how long these seven years must have felt for her, a physically unattractive woman with few prospects of a marriage partner, her tattered dreams and feelings of inferiority exposed and exacerbated every day.

Upon final payment of the dowry, Jacob demanded to be married to his long-awaited fiancée, but a devious plot twist was afoot. Trickster Laban brought the entire community together to celebrate the nuptials with a huge feast. A Middle Eastern custom during this period dictated that the bride remain completely silent and hidden behind a heavy veil during the ceremony, before quietly being escorted to her husband's bedchamber for the great unveiling.

After seven years, the honeymoon had commenced and Jacob assumed that he had his dream woman in his arms.

But with the revealing light of a new morning came the dizzying realization that his dream had become a nightmare. Rachel was not the woman in his arms. In a cunning switcharoo to make even the best illusionist envious, Leah had been substituted for her younger sister.

As a side note, I'm guessing that Jacob must have been rather intoxicated not to notice the sisterly differences. The Bible doesn't elaborate on this scene, so one can only imagine the colourful language shouted by Jacob at the discovery; the deceiver had himself been royally duped. How much time do you think elapsed before Jacob arrived at Laban's door with a few choice words, demanding an explanation?

Can you relate to a similar deception? We can become so enraged by an injustice perpetrated against us that we close our minds to the hurtful offences we inflict on others. Let me put it another way: we often excuse our own intentions with ample grace while judging another's actions against us very harshly.

The parable of the unmerciful servant in Matthew 18:21–35 paints this very scenario. One man is graciously forgiven several lifetimes of debt before almost immediately imprisoning an acquaintance for failing to pay back a few dollars. It's a sobering reminder that we are commanded to treat others with godly love, considering the immeasurable sacrifice Jesus has paid for us.

Laban justified his trickery by citing the cultural tradition. He then schemed further in suggesting that Jacob work another seven years for Rachel's hand as well. At this time, polygamy was considered acceptable according to God's law.

Take a moment to consider each woman's perspective in this debacle. Had Rachel been locked away in a castle somewhere during the first wedding, unable to reach her prince charming? If so, I'm guessing she was furious at her father, and possibly abusive towards Leah. From Leah's vantage point, she was covertly given in marriage, slept with her new husband under crazy circumstances, and likely harassed by her volatile younger sister. She was potentially shunned during the honeymoon week while Jacob desperately awaited his marriage to Rachel. No doubt Leah carried the unmistakeable knowledge that she was neither loved nor desired. Maybe Leah was just a pawn in her father's hands, but if she was a consenting party in the deception, it backfired horrendously and the multidimensional fallout was hers to endure.

With Laban's self-serving ultimatum, Jacob had little choice but to complete Leah's bridal week, then pay for the privilege of marrying Rachel by working another seven years. Imagine Leah, humiliated and scorned. She doesn't appear to have ever gained the affection of her husband. The Bible makes it crystal clear that Leah was the lesser loved of

Jacob's wives. Following Jacob's marriage to Rachel, we read that *"he loved Rachel more than Leah"* (Genesis 29:30, ESV). Another translation infers that he even hated Leah.

Throughout this dark and painful reality, Leah's unfavoured heart is contrasted against Rachel's voluptuous body. In the next bleak phase of her marriage, Leah further doubted God's love despite His unchanging character as the One who truly sees, hears and knows the deepest ache of our hearts.

Have you ever been in that place? Questioning God's love and care or knowing it intellectually but not experientially? I have. During the COVID-19 pandemic, my professional life didn't work out the way I imagined. I felt hurt, betrayed, and abandoned by leaders I had laboured alongside. Amidst my own anguish, a friend sent a profoundly helpful text that read "May God's voice be heard in the silence that surrounds you." What a beautiful reminder! Sometimes the world may reject you, but God, even though seemingly silent and distant, is ever-present and passionately orchestrating His loving plans for you, just as He did for Leah.

Take a few moments to hear and know the Lord's gentle voice speaking over you right now. He whispers:

> I have loved you with an everlasting love; I have drawn you with unfailing kindness. (Jeremiah 31:3)

> The steadfast love of the Lord never ceases; his mercies never come to an end; they are new every morning; great is your faithfulness. (Lamentations 3:22–23, ESV)

> But from eternity to eternity the Lord's faithful love is toward those who fear him, and his righteousness toward the grandchildren. (Psalm 103:17, CSB)

> The Lord is near to those who are discouraged; he saves those who have lost all hope. (Psalm 34:18, GNT)

Friends, we have a choice in these difficult seasons. We can continue rehearsing the enemy's lies and succumb to that dark path, or we can choose to listen to God's message of truth and hope that faithfully speaks into our questioning souls.

How Do You See the World?

This choice will always inform the construction or deconstruction of our worldview. Albert Mohler described a worldview as a

> set of ideas that make the world operational for us… We form a worldview and then the worldview forms us. Ultimately the wholeness of our truth can be traced to the fact that God is Himself the author of all truth.[4]

God gives every single person the opportunity to align themselves with His loving reality. We would all be wise to carefully evaluate our current worldview and assess its impact on us and through us. For example, when the challenges of life are beyond the scope of our control, where is our hope and confidence anchored? Is it grounded in the sure foundation of God? If so, the wind can blow, the waves can crash, and the rising floodwaters can threaten to overcome us, but His perfect love will forever hold us secure.

It's a reality of life that difficult things happen, and no one is exempt. In John 16:33, Jesus even said, *"In this world you will have trouble…"* However, He also adds a steadfast caveat to this disappointment: *"But take heart! I have overcome the world."* In other words, "Don't sweat it, because I'm forever with you in the storm providing a safe refuge." Remember Jehovah Shalom (the Lord our Peace). We must choose whether we are going to rest in His abiding promise of peace and honour this decision with praise.

Noted Christian psychologist Dr. Henry Cloud describes a failure to apprehend such uncontrollable circumstances as living with "learned helplessness." He shares that these will likely manifest in three interrelated

---

[4] Albert Mohler, *Conviction to Lead: 25 Principles for Leadership that Matters* (Ada, MI: Baker Publishing Group, 2014), 45.

dimensions: personally, pervasively, and permanently. Cloud's suggested antidote involves praising God as we navigate these seasons and asserting positive action over the areas in which we have control.

Furthermore, we should identify the complementary set of circumstances over which we have no specific jurisdiction and surrender these to the perfect sovereignty of our Father God who loves us more than we will ever know.

Put another way, the key to growing in divine wisdom is trusting God enough to give up control of what we cannot, positively impact the areas that we can, and praise Him in every circumstance. The Serenity Prayer, popularized by Reinhold Neibuhr, powerfully articulates this concept as a testimony of praise.[5]

Before Kristy and I were married in 2002, we made a mutual pact to spend a decade in each other's home countries to fully appreciate both sets of family, culture, and heritage. Following almost eleven years in Australia, we packed up our family and moved to Canada to complete the reciprocal part of our agreement.

We both had jobs in radiation therapy and our Canadian employer had verbally agreed to take us on once we arrived in British Columbia. However, we were stunned to learn that while we were in transit the province had instated a hiring freeze that indefinitely nullified our professional aspirations. This decision was entirely outside of our control and completely arrested our career trajectory, not to mention our income stream.

Given our palpable panic, we both began applying for work anywhere and everywhere to stabilize our immediate financial dilemma. Even though the clouds of worry swirled, God's faithfulness held us tight.

The only opportunity I could find was a minimum wage job at a local tourist attraction in Victoria, the spectacularly beautiful Butchart Gardens. I worked for five months pricing merchandise in an underground stockroom before transporting the merchandise upstairs for sale.

---

[5] "The Serenity Prayer: Applying 3 Truths from the Bible," *Crosswalk*. November 10, 2023 (www.crosswalk.com/faith/prayer/serenity-prayer-applying-3-truths-from-the-bible.html).

My personal disillusionment was further exacerbated when a fellow seasonal employee asked a confronting question: "You have two degrees in radiation therapy and counselling, right? So why are you working here?"

"Exactly!" I retorted under my breath.

The sting of this acknowledgement did little to comfort me—that is, until I began choosing to praise God and surrender my current desert season. During my time at Butchart Gardens, the Lord gently taught me to praise and trust His faithful direction even when I couldn't see the mysterious work of His hand. I was humbled to make godly deposits into the lives of several colleagues who were themselves weathering difficult storms in their current seasons with God's hope, life, and purpose.

God is forever perfect and we have the opportunity to praise His matchless goodness through every season.

What Do You See?

Our perspective is key to how we walk through each season. Moses demonstrated this principle throughout Exodus as he developed from shepherd to godly national leader. During his questions and doubts, he led his flock of sheep to the far side of the desert and had an unexpected encounter with the very same God who first spoke to Abram.

Exodus 3:1 records that Moses came to Horeb, a mountain whose name means "desert" or "desolation." The arid landscape perfectly mirrored Moses's current situation; he was just existing with a herd of bleating friends, trying to keep everyone fed while he was starved for purpose and direction.

An interesting detail about Horeb is that it also has an alternate name: Mount Sinai, the mountain of God. Several significant transformations happened here. God met Moses there, and later the prophet Elijah (1 Kings 19), in their own emptiness and fear. When we exhaust our options and can't see a way through, God even uses our dead ends to perform His miracle and propel us forward into the future He has uniquely crafted for us.

So the question beckons: how do you see the mountain ahead? Through the pain of your own perspective or through praise for God's sovereignty? In times of challenge, our bodies and emotions elevate a fearful reality and seek to distract us from choosing to embrace the truth of God's Word and character. I'm convinced that our most passionate and authentic praise testimony arises from our greatest pain, as God alone is both our Healer and Restorer. He never wastes any painful event. Given the overwhelming hurt and rejection of Leah's reality, her testimony would eventually declare that God's faithfulness forever sees, hears, and graciously responds to us in our seemingly hopeless situations.

Our awesome God is committed to showing everyone that He can be trusted with every part of our lives. He had a specific plan for Leah's journey, irrespective of whether Jacob preferred her, and He has the same goodness in His heart for you. His plan is to work all things together for our good as we choose to daily praise, surrender, and follow Jesus as Saviour and Lord (Romans 8:28).

And yes, my friend, God sees your heart, knows the specificity of your wounds, and promises to demonstrate His miracle-working power!

The choice comes back to us: are we ready and willing to exchange our Horeb experience for praising the Lord of Mount Sinai? We can begin right now by choosing to praise the Lord our God, the One who both created every mountain and oversees their existence.

Reflection Time

- Do you know the history behind your earthly name?

- Similar to Leah, how has your name, identity, pain points, or societal labels negatively impacted you in the past?

- Ephesians 2:10 testifies that you are God's masterpiece, and every masterpiece is named exclusively by its creator. Take a moment to ask God how He has named you and for what specific purpose.

- What is one thing you can do today to align with how your loving heavenly Father has named you?

2

Leah's First Son, Reuben
(BECAUSE #1)

> *Leah became pregnant and gave birth to a son. She named him Reuben, for she said, "It is because the Lord has seen my misery. Surely my husband will love me now."*
> (Genesis 29:32)

Ever heard the saying that misery loves company? While this is true, misery can also thrive in isolation—that is, if it goes unchallenged. Most people have found themselves here before. While this appears to have been Leah's prevailing disposition, I too have sporadically bought shares in this debilitating mindset. Maybe this is one reason her journey is so relatable to me. She's human, just like us, and many of her thoughts, actions, and responses are congruent with our own experiences, either historically or present day.

Let's dive into the story behind her pain.

For context, the cultural narrative of Genesis suggested that barrenness was understood as a punishment from God. Conversely, there was divine blessing upon those who could have offspring, especially sons, as males could carry the family name, serve as breadwinners, and support parents as they aged, were widowed, or became incapacitated.

The author of Genesis captures our Father's merciful heart so beautifully: *"When the Lord saw that Leah was not loved, he enabled her to conceive, but Rachel remained childless"* (Genesis 29:31). What a beautiful promise this is for us to remember. God sees and responds to our unique situations, including our deep distress. How often do we pause to notice the goodness of God amongst the challenges of life? While His answers may not always materialize in the way we hope, given our limited perspective, He always sees our pain and works with a goodness that transcends our understanding.

One of Leah's contemporaries experienced this principle amid her own crisis. Hagar was the Egyptian maidservant of Sarai, Abram's wife. She became a forced surrogate mother for Abram and Sarai as they tried to speed the arrival of the great nation God had promised them.

But God won't be rushed. Our attempts to manufacture human solutions usually culminate in a big mess. Unsurprisingly, that's exactly what happened here. Sarai was barren and concluded that Hagar should serve as her surrogate, as was culturally acceptable. I wonder if that duty was ever listed on Hagar's job description?

Abram agreed to Sarai's plan. When Hagar became pregnant, she began flaunting her ability to conceive over her mistress. As you'd imagine, this didn't go down too well and Abram was forced to intervene to preserve his marital harmony. With the power dynamic now flipped, Sarai mistreated Hagar. As a result, Hagar fled into the desert to find refuge elsewhere.

Frightened and alone, the Lord's angel found Hagar sitting beside a desert spring. After voicing her pain, she was commanded by God to return home and faithfully submit to Sarai.

Further details were revealed about her son's destiny and in response she spoke a divine revelation that continues to resonate strongly in my spirit: *"She gave this name to the Lord who spoke to her: 'You are the God who sees me,' for she said, 'I have now seen the One who sees me'"* (Genesis 16:13). What a profound response! From the depth of her pain, Hagar said of her Provider, "You see me, You see my need, and You've orchestrated an answer that far surpasses the problem."

Hagar's God, who transcends time and space, is the same God we praise today. Our God of love and mercy also sees you, loves you, and is responding to your needs with the same perpetually caring passion. Let's praise Him for His goodness!

Okay, God, but...

Leah's story has many notable similarities to Hagar's. This broken woman benefitted from God seeing her dire predicament of a loveless marriage and provided a tangible reminder of His unfailing presence.

As we will see in the coming chapters, three boys were born to Leah, three divine gifts, yet Leah made three excuses for their manifestation which partially overshadowed the kindness of God's blessing. From Leah's perspective, I wonder whether she may have been ruminating on my own reworked lyrics from the old hymn "Blessed Assurance":

> Blessed excuses, oh pitiful me.
> God's gift in three babies, to pacify me.

Each baby boy born to Leah can be juxtaposed against the backdrop of her tainted marriage and deep insecurity. This is clearly seen in the children's names, each of which correlates with the depth of her pain and the failing hope she clung to in her goal of gaining favour with Jacob.

Leah's first son was named Reuben, which means "see, a son." Hats off to Leah for her creativity and the ability to recognize gender! In the Hebrew, however, this name translates to misery. While I don't seek to make jokes at Leah's expense, what else would you expect? A guy known for his deception had a child with a physically flawed and deeply broken woman who existed in a dysfunctional marital triangle with her envious sister. What other meaning would you expect than misery?

In our self-centred society, gratitude and contentment aren't always celebrated when God's goodness intersects with our pain.

Leah justified her attitude towards this first gift by saying, *"It is because the Lord has seen my misery. Surely my husband will love me now"* (Genesis 29:32). Have you ever noticed how our vocabulary can lend so much insight into our heart posture? Jesus made this truth clear when He said to a large crowd of followers and spectators, *"Your words show what is in your heart"* (Luke 6:45, CEV).

From the word "because" in Leah's statement, we know the blame game is about to start. But to be fair, how fast do we make accusations and seek to blame everyone but ourselves? Though Leah didn't directly implicate God, she probably wasn't too happy with Him either. It may surprise you, but He isn't in the business of manipulating our feelings to orchestrate sustainable transformation in our lives. He doesn't sovereignly enrol us into His school of divine behaviour modification or spiritual cognitive behavioural therapy. It's just not His MO. Instead He repeatedly shows us His grace-filled nature, His flawless character, and invites us to make an informed choice about our trajectory that either aligns with or rejects His goodness.

In reflecting on my own journey, I'm so thankful for my parents' regular encouragement for me to remember what God is doing now and has done in the past to help me live consistently with His promises as my anchor. The alternative is feeling like victims of our changing circumstances and fluctuating feelings.

While growing up, during our evening meal Mum and Dad would have us kids share about the blessings of God we'd noticed that day. The monotony seemed boring compared to my friends' opportunity to watch TV during dinner, but I can now appreciate how this helped me maintain an internal dossier to remember God's faithfulness in my life.

I would strongly encourage all Jesus-followers to maintain diligent records of His faithful orchestration. This consistent practice helps us to trust Him with tomorrow's challenges based on yesterday's historical precedent while praising Him today.

Some Painful Questions

The pursuit of gratitude and contentment is a principle addressed in a book by Russ Harris entitled *The Happiness Trap*. In it, Harris asserts that people spend relentless energy seeking happiness and avoiding unhappy scenarios. He poses an interesting question by asking, "What if your very efforts to find happiness were actually preventing you from achieving it?"[6]

Viewing this question through a biblical lens, we must ask: what if an excessive focus on ourselves hinders us from praising God through our lives and prevents us from experiencing the joy associated with this discipline? Sometimes we're so intent on looking everywhere else but God to meet the deepest needs of the soul. In such scenarios, we exchange our longing for God with envy for people or things. The outcome makes happiness a conditional moving target.

The world can throw us off-course in demanding that we covet more instead of being content with the abundance that's freely available to us in the person of Jesus. The enemy of our souls uses envy to great effect by enticing us to believe the lie that someone else's journey is far more fulfilling than ours. We feel tempted to resist the lessons God is seeking to teach us here and now for our own benefit.

Comparison can likewise be a silent thief that steals our joy and undermines our intimacy with our loving heavenly Father. It causes us to criticize instead of celebrate. Comparison traps always end up reinforcing the same conclusion: we will never be good enough, smart enough, wealthy enough, attractive enough, powerful enough, or special enough.

In stark contrast, God loves us for the unique individuals He created us to be and invites us to live passionately within this reality. We are encouraged in 1 Peter 5:6–7 to *"be content with who you are, and don't put on airs. God's strong hand is on you; he'll promote you at the right time. Live carefree before God; he is most careful with you"* (MSG). So as we learn to focus our praise on the Giver instead of our subjective assessment of our deficit, we find abundance in our relationship with the God of eternal hope, life, and joy.

In a related question, have you ever been guilty of desiring the blessings of God more than the person of God? Influenced by consumer culture, Abram certainly was. Having already received God's promise of future generations and unfailing protection, he fell into a common trap; he held God in contempt. Genesis 15:1–3 narrates some relatable dialogue between the duo:

---

[6] Russ Harris, *The Happiness Trap* (Boulder, CO: Shambhala Publications, 2008), 1.

After this, the word of the Lord came to Abram in a vision: "Do not be afraid, Abram. I am your shield, your very great reward."

But Abram said, "Sovereign Lord, what can you give me since I remain childless and the one who will inherit my estate is Eliezer of Damascus?"

And Abram said, "You have given me no children; so a servant in my household will be my heir."

God said to Abram, "I've got you, mate." I am your protection and everything you need." To which Abram responded, "Ahhh… your *everything* just isn't enough to meet my current needs and future dreams. I need children to be happy—and right now, my lineage ends with me. So no, Your providence just isn't enough right now."

Sound familiar? Though our situations are likely different, our pain and brokenness can obscure God's goodness both to us and through us. Though He never leaves us, our clouded perspective towards His purpose can lead us to live far below the purpose to which He calls us.

There is no doubting that hurt, pain, and the questions of life are very real. The writer of Psalm 102 knew this all too well, writing, *"Do not hide your face from me when I am in distress. Turn your ear to me; when I call, answer me quickly"* (Psalm 102:2). I can only imagine what the psalmist was experiencing to write this deep heart cry.

Jesus also understood this pain, even more than we'll ever know. Hanging on a Roman cross, having endured pain beyond comprehension, He cried out to His Father amidst the sin-fractured reality of their intimate relationship: *"My God, my God, why have you abandoned me?"* (Matthew 27:46, NLT)

But praise Jesus, our Saviour and Lord, this was not the end of the story. Three days later, He rose from death, having conquered the grave, and now sits at the right hand of our Father God. He now advocates to the Father on our behalf. Hebrews 4:15 validates this truth: *"For we do not have a high priest who is unable to empathize with our weaknesses, but we have one who has been tempted in every way, just as we are—yet he did not sin."*

The hurt and pain of this life can lead us towards depression and death, but God transforms these realities by inviting us into the very presence of Jesus for help and hope.

Friend, wherever you are on life's journey, you are loved beyond measure with the steadfast promise that Father God will never let you go. His grace proves itself most profoundly in that He wants to embrace and empower us, despite our weakness, problems, and mess.

Yes, you heard right: God's ability to save and restore is more than enough for anyone who chooses to humbly surrender to Him.

The Reuben Issue

Let's return to Leah, who was busy focusing on the craving she felt she desperately needed yet didn't possess: the love of Jacob. While her desire wasn't entirely wrong, this focus became an idol that stood above the infinite love God already had for her.

Without the clarity of God's truth, we can allow the cultural narrative of society or the ache in our own hearts to dictate our hopes, values, and direction. The key to escaping this deadly paradigm is knowing who we are in Christ, knowing our divinely customized purpose and committing to following this trajectory irrespective of the prevailing circumstances.

Many verses speak to this truth, like 1 Peter 2:9, which emphatically proclaims, *"But you are a chosen people, a royal priesthood, a holy nation, God's special possession, that you may declare the praises of him who called you out of darkness into his wonderful light."*

God wrote His unchanging love and truth for each of us with the blood of Jesus. The Bible speaks of it and creation testifies to it, but it's our personal responsibility to apprehend this truth and live consistently in its reality. Sometimes our emotions rob us of such profound facts and deceive us into believing the lie that we are somehow excluded from His all-inclusive invitation.

But we have a choice. Instead of becoming imprisoned as helpless victims of our own emotions, we can start to employ practical habits that pivot our mental trajectory from hopeless resignation to the realization that we have an active voice in the trajectory of our lives.

Take a few moments to imagine all the hurtful words, negative thoughts, destructive lies, and societal narratives circulating in your head, all of which are mixing with the hope of God's truth. Is it any wonder that we end up with hearts full of confusion punctuated with dashed hopes? We allow God's truth to become so diluted.

Holocaust survivor and psychiatrist Viktor Frankl wrote something profound: "between the stimulus and the response there is a space, and in that space is your power and your freedom."[7] The space of which Frankl speaks is the point when we pause to choose what happens next. Like the operators of a dam, who can control whether a downstream city gets flooded, we have the opportunity to invite the Holy Spirit to be our gatekeeper of God's experiential truth, thus impacting our lives.

For this reason, the amour of God is an incredibly powerful defensive and offensive weapon. The apostle Paul wrote in Ephesians 6:10–18 of the divine equipment given to Jesus-followers to overcome the devil's schemes. These include the belt of truth (to know His mind), the breastplate of righteousness (to protect our hearts), the shoes of God (to keep us moving on our divine mission), the shield of faith (to extinguish the enemy's fiery salvos), His helmet of salvation (to remind us of whose we are), and the sword of the Spirit, God's Word (to know Him and His purpose in and through us). We must never forget to communicate with God directly through prayer and praise, with the Holy Spirit's assistance.

We have a choice about what we listen to and the messages we harbour as truth. We were not created to be preprogrammed robots. Our loving heavenly Father has entrusted this autonomy to every person, and it coexists with the ever-present reality of His daily goodness in our lives.

Yet with this autonomy comes personal responsibility and accountability for our own spiritual decisions and trajectory.

To this point, Hagar's pregnancy resulted in the birth of a man called Ishmael. He was born into similar circumstances to those experienced by Leah and Rachel; he was raised by two jealous women and a father suffering decisional paralysis.

---

[7] "Alleged Quote," *Viktor Frankl*. Date of access: August 2, 2025 (https://www.viktorfrankl.org/quote_stimulus.html).

Though much of what happened to Ishmael as a boy cannot be blamed on him, his own choices as an adult perpetuated the problem. He didn't become an active part of God's solution. He chose to live under his own circumstances rather than embrace godly obedience to transcend them.

This is the same choice we must all make, which includes our decision towards praise. Though we may be thrust into some challenging circumstances, we can always decide how to respond.

How's Your Eyesight?

Ever heard the saying "seeing is believing"? While this is true in many earthly scenarios, it's certainly not a Kingdom principle. Looking through the eyes of God's steadfast promises gives us the ability to see His pathways beyond the immediate challenges of our three-dimensional environment.

The story is told of Walt Disney's widow Lillian being a guest of honour at the opening of Walt Disney World in 1971. As she stood onstage, the friend beside her quipped that it was a shame Walt wasn't there to see the unveiling. Lillian's response? "He did see it. That's why it now exists!"

How true this is! If we merely live based on what we can see with our limited visual senses, we miss so much of the richness God has for us.

So let me invite you to do something different. What would happen if you asked God to open your spiritual eyes to see what He has made available?

In the book of 2 Kings, Elisha's servant recounts the effect of his mentor's prayer. Elisha and the servant stood surrounded by what the Bible describes as a strong enemy force of horses, chariots, and a detachment of soldiers sent by the king of Aram to secure their capture. God's miracle-working power was put on display as the unnamed servant woke early one morning, panic-stricken to see such a formidable army surrounding the city.

One translation captures the servant's extremely anxious response to his master by repeatedly using a four-letter word. The Douay-Rheims

Bible records him saying, *"Alas, alas, alas, my lord, what shall we do?"* (2 Kings 6:15, DRA)

Elisha responded calmly, and with similar words to the ones Jesus later used to comfort his disciples.

> But [Elisha] answered: Fear not: for there are more with us than with them.
> And [Elisha] prayed, and said: Lord, open his eyes, that he may see. And the Lord opened the eyes of the servant, and he saw: and behold the mountain was full of horses, and chariots of fire round about [Elisha]. (2 Kings 6:16–17, DRA)

Between our human fear and God's amazing answers stands the invitation of faith and praise. Prolific author Phillip Yancey penned this phrase: "faith means trusting in advance what will only make sense in reverse."[8] Faith is what sustains the Jesus-follower when they're afraid, shocked, and paralyzed by life's circumstances. Faith is what activates and mobilizes the vision God has placed in our hearts.

The book of Hebrews vigorously exhorts us to *"fix our eyes on Jesus, the author and perfecter of our faith"* (Hebrews 12:2, BSB) in order to access God's glory, which far exceeds the temporal challenges we face. Paul adds to this divine revelation, saying, *"No eye has seen, no ear has heard, and no mind has imagined what God has prepared for those who love him"* (1 Corinthians 2:9, NLT).

A beautiful symbiotic relationship is found when we look with eyes of faith and cultivate a lifestyle of praise. The choice to praise fuels our faith, and faith in action reciprocally spurs praise. Neither can exist without the other.

I strongly encourage you to choose to praise God and allow His faith to rise within your spirit.

Our awesome heavenly Father knows the situations you're navigating and has lovingly gone ahead to prepare the way. He knows our thoughts

---

[8] Philip Yancey, "The Long View," *Philip Yancey*. June 2023 (https://philipyancey.com/the-long-view).

and encourages us to renew our minds in the unchanging knowledge of His good, pleasing, and perfect will, which progressively transforms our limited and flawed perspective. He knows our weakness and promises to give us strength and courage for the journey. God's divine invitation echoes throughout eternity, assuring us that our *"momentary troubles are achieving for us an eternal glory that far outweighs them all. So we fix our eyes not on what is seen, but on what is unseen, since what is seen is temporary, but what is unseen is eternal"* (2 Corinthians 4:17–18).

The Validity of Pain

In speaking to the Leah inside us who legitimately laments the misery of so much pain, let me encourage you not to simply dwell in your present reality. Crises have an innate way of amplifying the belief systems we hold as sacred. We can write a negative self-fulfilling prophecy and actively work towards its manifestation and proliferation.

Alternatively, Christ-followers can choose to view their trials through the hope-filled lens of Scripture, which is faithful in the storm, instead of being tossed about by their changing feelings or seasonal opinions.

Some Christians are trapped in debilitating mental prisons, living each day as slaves to their own relativistic thoughts instead of choosing to praise and take these realities captive by making them obedient to Christ's faith-filled promises. Paul's letter, written to the early church in Colosse, implored them—and us—towards this godly perspective: *"continue to live your lives in him, rooted and built up in him, strengthened in the faith as you were taught, and overflowing with thankfulness"* (Colossians 2:6–7).

Where the Rubber Hits the Road

As we praise God in faith, some practical applications include the concept of *thought replacement*, a psychological staple that ultimately has deep biblical roots, as seen in Colossians 3:2, which exhorts us, *"Think about the things of heaven, not the things of earth"* (NLT).

For each challenging situation in which you find yourself, identify a verse you can look at often to extinguish the enemy's lies. The concordance in the back of many Bibles is extremely helpful for researching verses on topics like peace, hope, or refuge, to name just a few examples. Or search online for a verse or song which you can use to anchor yourself during such seasons and praise God's goodness as your faith is strengthened.

Another suggestion is to create a digital resilience album, which you can look at when times become overwhelming. My cellphone now contains a growing library of encouraging verses, inspiring photos, life events, edifying testimonies, and helpful poems that all point back to God's faithful promises. I use them as a praise-igniter to rehearse His goodness of the past and remind myself that He doesn't change; I can trust in His unfailing character both today and tomorrow.

Maybe you want to journal and regularly record what God shows you in order to remember His historical faithfulness. I know a family that chooses to write out and store God's blessings in a jar. At the end of each year, they empty the jar, read the blessings aloud, and celebrate what He has done as a microcosm of what He is doing on a macroscale.

Praising God could involve a personalized song or poem that you create in celebration of who He is. Or you could bask in the magnificence of His creation during a walk to remind yourself of how great God is. Seeing God through the eyes of faith is a daily and active choice compared to the default of living as a circumstantial victim.

A friend of mine, Kevin, was once caught in the difficult situation of being evicted from a rented house. He and his family were forced to quickly find another place in a low-inventory market due to the owner's snap decision to sell. This was almost impossible!

However, Kevin stood resolute and said, "I am not going to wait for the manifestation of God's answer before I start praising Him for what I see through the eyes of faith."

He and his family started celebrating and rehearsing God's faithfulness in advance of the answer. Approximately five months later, God miraculously provided a house they have since purchased.

Is this story incredible? Well, not really. Miracles are just the nature of our God's character. This time, let's choose to praise God and see Him through eyes of faith.

Reflection Time

- Do you share Leah's perspective that God owes you? Maybe you feel as though He gave "your" deserved opportunity, dream job, necessary cure, or long-awaited pregnancy to someone else. How has this coloured your daily faith journey?

- The practices of blame and coveting can be closely related. How might ruminating on these issues illuminate a barrier or void in your life?

- Take a moment to think about how God has seen and responded to a unique need in your past. Ask for His wisdom to remind you of a situation you've long since forgotten.

- Spend two minutes praising God as the One who sees you (El Roi, Genesis 16:13–14) and offer a short prayer like this one: "God, may Your word take root in my life today. Help me see Your hand, know Your heart, and praise Your sovereignty."

3

Leah's Second Son, Simeon
(BECAUSE #2)

> *She conceived again, and when she gave birth to a son she said, "Because the Lord heard that I am not loved, he gave me this one too." So she named him Simeon.*
> (Genesis 29:33)

March 2020 marked the beginning of a very different season for the entire global community. The terms "pandemic" and "COVID-19" made their way into every conversation from national addresses to dinner table banter. Few could have guessed the implications, magnitude, or duration of what lay ahead.

The practical stopgap measure of social distancing was enforced in many communities—and like with many other businesses and organizations, the church staff I was part of was told to work from home for the foreseeable future to curb the disease's spread.

Driving home that day, the city of Victoria, normally a thriving metropolis, felt like a ghost town. Everyone was required to adopt isolative practices, making even neighbourhood walks rather lonely experiences as friends and strangers alike moved apart to create a bubble of safety around themselves under the assumption that many were infected with this prolific disease.

Living with my wife and two teenagers felt rather restrictive during this time, and I could only imagine the isolation experienced by those who lived alone. Mother Teresa was once quoted as saying, "Loneliness and the feeling of being unwanted is the most terrible poverty."[9]

I wonder if this forlorn statement could also have spilled from Leah's heart. How long had she been Jacob's wife? Two or three years, I would guess. That's a long time to live devoid of affection. Oh sure, there was likely some sexual engagement with Jacob, either for personal physical gratification or reproduction, but this was far from what Leah ultimately desired. She had two healthy sons, but she remained impoverished by loneliness and barren in love.

Though your situation may be very different, Leah's prevailing sentiment could be quite relatable, with haunting memories that play on a mental loop and stab at the heart time after time.

Several other Bible personalities would nod in sober acknowledgement too. Joseph, one of Jacob's sons, would be a prime example—betrayed, falsely accused, imprisoned, hopeless, dejected, and wondering when justice would ever prevail.

Yet a beautiful refrain is repeated thrice in Joseph's story, and it echoes through his scriptural testimony: *"the Lord was with Joseph"* (Genesis 39:2, 21, 23).

The same is true for you. Let me say it clearly, and please take a moment for this truth to sink in: the God of the universe always sees you and hears you! He invites you to trust Him, even though you may not be able to perceive what He's working on behind the scenes, and fortify your resolve with praise.

Pastor and author Shaun Nepstead draws an intriguing analogy in his book, *Don't Quit in the Dip*. He refers to a painting, entitled "Checkmate," which depicts an existential competition between a man

---

[9] "Saints Among Us: The Work of Mother Teresa," *Time*. December 29, 1975 (https://time.com/archive/6878542/saints-among-us-the-work-of-mother-teresa).
Mother Teresa, "Article," *Time Magazine*. December 29, 1975.

and the devil, with the game's outcome determining the mortal's eternal destination.

Deeply intrigued by this piece of artwork, an accomplished chess master and art connoisseur took the time to reconstruct the current state of play with a borrowed chessboard. He then passionately uttered,

> Young man in the painting, I sure wish you could hear me right now, because I've got some good news. The devil only thinks he has won, but I've been studying the board, and there is a move he has missed! If you could see what I see, the whole nature of this game would change.[10]

The same is true for us. With Jesus rising from the dead, humanity's eternal freedom is celebrated with a triumphant shout. This is a move the devil grossly underestimated. That same power exists for everyone who confesses Jesus as Saviour and Lord.

King David, who arose from Leah's lineage, would later join in the victory chorus, scribing many psalms detailing his struggles before climaxing with exuberant praise for God's powerful interventions. Listen to his heart on vivid display in Psalm 18:6: *"In my distress I called to the Lord; I cried to my God for help. From his temple he heard my voice; my cry came before him, into his ears."*

Yes, my friends, God always hears our pleas. Another passage ratifies God's desire to hear us. He says, *"When you call on me, when you come and pray to me, I'll listen. When you come looking for me, you'll find me"* (Jeremiah 29:12–13, MSG).

God's Message in the Pain

It's curious that the Hebrew name for Simeon translates as "one who hears." Undoubtedly, some of the biggest questions for Christ-followers, and those curious about this worldview, include:

---

[10] Shaun Nepstad, *Don't Quit in the Dip* (Franklin, TN: Worthy Books, 2023), 4.

- Does God hear me?
- Is He even listening?
- With all the people and events in human history, does He even know my name?

Leah likely struggled with these same doubts. She gave God a backhanded compliment when naming her second son: *"Because the Lord heard that I am not loved, he gave me this one too"* (Genesis 29:33).

Simeon's name can arguably be viewed in a few different ways. With Leah's first son, she said that the Lord *saw* she was not loved and gave her a son as a substitute. With her second son, Leah said that God had *heard* that she was unloved, so He gave another son to placate her.

Were these children token blessings to appease her, or were they the tangible manifestation of something far more profound God was orchestrating in her life?

The famous author C.S. Lewis highlights a divine methodology at play, writing, "God whispers to us in our pleasures, speaks to us in our conscience, but shouts in our pain; it is His megaphone to rouse a deaf world."[11] Pain, though often uncomfortable, is a tool God uses to transcend the surrounding noise—until we can clearly hear His continuous message of love.

My own multidimensional pain reached fever pitch in September 2009. After tenaciously battling leukaemia for eighteen long months, my amazing dad, a godly mentor and irreplaceable friend, transitioned from this earth into the loving embrace of our heavenly Father. Our family had stood resolute in praying and believing for God's healing, yet in that moment I felt like I had been betrayed. Had God even heard our cries? And if so, then why this outcome?

There were no words to express the hurt. All I could think to say was "God, You stay right there until I need you. I don't want you right now. I just want my dad back."

Every night prior, Kristy and I had prayed with our kids before bed. But after Dad's passing, I distinctly remember saying to Kristy, "You pray for now. I'll just respond with a hollow amen." Consumed by pain,

---

[11] C.S. Lewis, *The Problem of Pain* (London, UK: Geoffrey Bles, Centenary Press, 1946), 82.

I wasn't listening to God and didn't care to hear Him; I just wanted Him to hear what He had failed to do and its profound impact on me.

During this turmoil, I received some valuable advice from a counselling professor who assured me that God was big enough to hold my raw anger.

For the next six months, the Hound of Heaven gently yet respectfully pursued me as I processed this pain—that is, until I was finally ready to make peace with the outcome and actively re-engage in my Christian faith journey.

Many years have since passed, and I know more than ever that praise in its multitude of forms elevates the One who holds us securely in His hands, even as our tears fall. God's heart beats for us, and that heartbeat is even more real than the pain that seeks to engulf us. The choice and timing lie within our grasp. So when you're ready, reach out your hand to release the anger and take hold of His peace through praise.

Are You Listening?

"Are you listening?"

"Yes," I responded alongside my classmates.

Our elementary teacher was confirming that she had our undivided attention.

Since then, I've wondered whether we ask the same of God, albeit in our more sophisticated adult ways, as validation that the Lord hears us when we pray.

Are there times when you've wondered whether the cries of our hearts simply fade into oblivion? Like Leah, I have. But listen to the psalmist and stand resolute with his contention: *"I love the Lord because he hears my voice and my prayer for mercy. Because he bends down to listen, I will pray as long as I have breath!"* (Psalm 116:1–2, NLT) What beautiful imagery of the sovereign Lord who holds dominion among limitless universes and yet chooses to bend down and listen to every individual, not simply to hear our spoken words but also every silent whisper, unformed hope, unspeakable pain and inexpressible hurt!

He does this for you today too. And while you may not feel heard, that doesn't extinguish the truth of this biblical fact.

Given this assertion, let me pause and pose a related question: if God hears me, why doesn't He answer in the way I ask? Maybe this pain is what enveloped Leah as she wrestled while raising her two dependant sons devoid of Jacob's affection.

Here again arises a reality in the Christian faith: we often have a consumer-style relationship with God's hand instead of fostering an intimate relationship with His heart.

A few years ago, I was in a hurry to grab a few staples from the grocery store. Running down the aisles, possibly knocking other shoppers out of the way, I took what I needed and then sent a selfish arrow prayer skyward. You know the type: "God, I need a parking spot close to the mall entrance. God, I need good weather today for my hiking adventure. God, I need a passing grade on this exam to get into my future career."

For me, it was: "God, I need an available grocery clerk to get me out of here pronto."

From the end of the aisle, I saw an empty register and hurriedly completed the fifty-meter sprint in record time towards my "heavenly answer." But as I rounded the corner, another shopper arrived there first. In my frustration, I concluded that God had dropped the ball.

After my emotions had subsided, I felt remorseful over this childish interaction. I had foolishly slandered God's goodness because He hadn't met my immediate and subjective demand. In our pain and confusion, we can allow feelings to inform our perspective and reinforce our distorted mindsets, without even giving God the right of reply.

The prophet Isaiah issued an important rebuke for such a contortion of truth:

> What sorrow awaits those who argue with their Creator. Does a clay pot argue with its maker? Does the clay dispute with the one who shapes it, saying, "Stop, you're doing it wrong!" Does the pot exclaim, "How clumsy can you be?" (Isaiah 45:9 NLT)

Have you ever told God that He was wrong and His plans were a mistake? I have, several times, in painful situations related to past jobs, health crises, and broken relationships.

The enemy of our souls uses deceit to stoke these fires towards a dangerous downward spiral of patterns and behaviours. We can't allow this to go unchecked. Allowing Satan the freedom to speak negativity into our depleted hearts carries the risk of producing relational distance between our hearts and God.

Another sinister tactic of the devil is self-counsel in isolation. He can use this to great effect in separating God's children from the Good Shepherd so that he can steal, kill, and destroy them. Some people misguidedly refer to this mental rumination as "processing," but these destructive thought patterns are generally unhelpful and can paint us into a corner if we fail to recognize and act against this endless rut.

Maybe this is your heart posture right now. Are you questioning His methodology? If so, let me gently encourage you to suspend this line of thinking and consider God's perspective. A few chapters later in Isaiah's discourse, God says,

> My thoughts are nothing like your thoughts… and my ways are far beyond anything you could imagine. For just as the heavens are higher than the earth, so my ways are higher than your ways and my thoughts higher than your thoughts. (Isaiah 55:8–9, NLT)

I appreciate that this truth won't solve many unanswerable questions on this side of eternity, but praise isn't based on our understanding or agreement with what God allows. Instead it's about bending our will towards Adoni, our Lord and Master who reigns supreme above our questions.

Taking a Knee

Our son spent five years playing junior soccer in Australia and Canada. It was fun and generally enjoyable. After many training nights in the bitter cold, however, when a warm shower and hot chocolate were required to bring his body temperature back to normal, he decided to hang up his cleats.

During this season of our lives, I discovered a valuable practice taught amongst North American players after a player is injured on the field. They all bend down on one knee to signify respect for the downed athlete and facilitate faster treatment.

This represents a necessary counterpoint to our self-reliant "processing." It is the humble posture of surrender, laying down our rights and demands and trusting the infinite wisdom of God's loving direction.

In Exodus 21 and Deuteronomy 15, God gave Moses His edict about freeing house servants and slaves from captivity after they had served their master for six years. In the seventh year, their earthly overlord was to release them with a generous supply from the abundance with which God had blessed them.

Yet this edict came with a remarkable caveat for any servant who decided that their future would be better spent in the continuous service of their earthly master:

> But if your servant says to you, "I do not want to leave you," because he loves you and your family and is well off with you, then take an awl and push it through his earlobe into the door, and he will become your servant for life. Do the same for your female servant. (Deuteronomy 15:16–17)

What an incredible realization of love that informs one's decision to surrender. The question remains: will we offer God our surrendered praise, firmly believing that we are well-off in His loving hands? Psalm 63:3 celebrates the psalmist's experience, saying, *"Your unfailing love is better than life itself; how I praise you!"* (NLT) If this is your desire and heart cry too, know that He is preparing you in every season of challenge for a joy that will far outshine the present suffering.

Don't allow your mind to camp on the lie that God isn't listening, or that He's forgotten you or is ignoring your pain. Instead choose to bloom where you are planted and live in the truth that God can do far more with our surrender than we can.

Now please don't mishear me—trials, hurt, pain, and overwhelming emotion are very real. But while we walk through these seasons, God is inviting into growth, not forcing us towards divine submission. Psalm 23:4 speaks of walking *"through the deepest darkness"* (GNT) instead of setting up camp and living there. It's about more than mere survival. Sometimes we don't walk through such seasons in ways that honour God or benefit us. We can deploy survival tactics and coping mechanisms to deaden the pain or delay what seems inevitable. In doing so, we can simultaneously block our ability to experience God's gift of salvation and abundant life, a gift that Jesus purchased through His death and resurrection.

We can find God's fingerprints of purpose over everything He allows and redeems. The author of Ecclesiastes testifies, *"To everything there is a season, and a time for every purpose under heaven"* (Ecclesiastes 3:1, BSB).

In his book *Live, Love, Lead*, pastor Brian Houston writes that

> as much as we may not like or understand it, everything means all the painful, unexpected, disappointing, frightening, challenging moments as well as the joyful, predictable, exciting, reassuring, and comfortable ones. Life includes our times of pain, of mourning and grieving, of suffering and healing and of fighting and reconciling.[12]

When the storms of life hit, our faith in Jesus needs to be founded on trust and praise versus any determination to understand why. While our trust may not automatically elicit a praise response, this too is a choice along the journey. The martyred disciple Peter said, *"Be glad for the chance to suffer as Christ suffered. It will prepare you for even greater happiness when he makes his glorious return"* (1 Peter 4:13, CEV).

Through this intentional decision, our trust and praise testify with confidence that God knows what He is doing. Jesus has already walked

---

[12] Brian Houston, *Live, Love, Lead* (Sydney, NSW: HarperCollins Publishers, 2015), 89.

this road ahead of us and the Holy Spirit empowers us with everything we need to walk it in a manner worthy of our high calling.

HIS PLANS FOR YOU ARE GOOD

Job is another Bible friend with whom we might identify when it comes to holding onto hope through disastrous events. He seemed to have it all. Then, within moments, all was taken away. His ten children perished, his servants were slaughtered, and several thousand livestock were killed. His relationship with his wife crumbled and his own health was compromised.

This would have been incredibly difficult to fathom. In a similar situation, our minds might go down a thousand dark rabbit holes.

Yet amid his lament and questions, we see Job's repentance and praise in his confession of humility to God, his Creator and Sustainer: *"Surely I spoke of things I did not understand, things too wonderful for me to know… My ears have heard of you but now my eyes have seen you"* (Job 42:3, 5).

During this man's challenging transformation, he relinquished the God he thought he knew and opened the door to embrace the God who truly is. This is what we are called to also: to trust and praise the God of truth irrespective of our circumstances.

Both Job and Leah parallel our lived human experience. While we stand in the confusing gap between who we are and all that God calls us to become, we find a place where God's divine growth happens in and through us. This divinely ordained holding tank prepares us to receive the fulfilment of His promise. It could be called a *liminal space*, from the Latin word *limen*, which can be defined as a threshold. Biblically, this translates to the holy ground that God uses as a staging area during our spiritual maturation. It often feels like a space of stretching and discomfort, of waiting while not yet knowing. This is an ideal place to practice the invitation to praise.

Job and Leah have compelling testimonies that invite us into a similar space of heartfelt praise, where we can say, *"The Lord is near to all who call on him, to all who call on him in truth. He fulfills the desires of those who fear him; he also hears their cry and saves them"* (Psalm 145:18–19, ESV).

A Humble Grape Vine

What godly dreams and desires are you wrestling with? What has He spoken into your heart to guard until they are fulfilled in His timing? Protect them carefully with His praise while holding them loosely. These dreams can often feel larger than our perceived capacity to hold them. Or maybe we don't believe we possess the necessary faith to see them through. Maybe we harbour overwhelming emotions that have coerced us into devaluing or even abandoning such dreams. Do we now exist devoid of God-given purpose, plagued by the regret of what might have been?

But your loving heavenly Father never condemns any such actions. This is the signature of our enemy, the thief and liar. While Satan would label this as a failure and hold it over our heads like a trophy, this seeming failure is never God's final destination for you. His love, mercy, and grace are forever deeper, higher, and wider—enough to cover any mistakes, intentional or unintentional, as we give Him this permission.

A great friend and spiritual mentor shared with me about a God vision he and his wife received in the 1980s. Bentley and his wife Sharon received an exciting impression about repurposing a small castle and adjoining vineyard in the south of France which they called the Chateau of Peace. They sensed that this opportunity had been designed for them to develop a place of refreshment and restoration for missionaries and pastors recuperating from the demands of ministry before continuing their kingdom work.

Yet thirty-five years after receiving the dream, they still hadn't witnessed its physical manifestation. Some would find this long delay extremely disheartening. But with a beautifully anchored spirit of praise, Bentley shared with me his evolving wisdom.

"Over time we've discovered that it's more about who you are called to become than what you are called to do," he told me. "The Chateau of Peace became a huge driver for so long, but in God's wisdom and mercy He showed us that we are the Chateau of Peace. We have it, live in it, and minister out of it because of Him."

The sovereign Author of these plans had spoken the dream to them and He progressively built it for His purpose, praise, and glory through them.

With an engaging laugh, Bentley went on to share about God's sense of humour during the long wait. Years ago, this couple had purchased a house in Victoria complete with terraced gardens and one measly grape vine in a small garden that definitely didn't resemble the vineyard from the dream. Bentley joked that God knew He had to start him off small.

Instead of becoming embittered about this humble starting point, Bentley faithfully tended to his singular vine. While enjoying the horticultural process, his spiritual learning became incredibly rich. With each dry Victorian summer, the plant's roots grew robust, tunnelling deep in search of water and nutrients. Vintners refer to this process as *stressing* the vine, a process which injects maximum energy into developing fruit to concentrate the sugar levels and increase the complexity of flavour.

After diligently tending to the vine for a decade of scorching temperatures and drought conditions, this single vine produced the most plentiful and delicious harvest. Praise, tenacity, diligence and thanksgiving are generously mixed throughout Bentley's testimony. He and Sharon continue to see God's goodness in action.

Jeremiah 17:7–8 confirms the spiritual principle that aligns with Bentley's lived experience:

> Blessed is the man who trusts in the Lord, whose trust is the Lord. He is like a tree planted by water, that sends out its roots by the stream, and does not fear when heat comes, for its leaves remain green, and is not anxious in the year of drought, for it does not cease to bear fruit. (ESV)

In hearing God's perfectly customized invitation for you, choose to trust Him and send out spiritual roots with praise irrespective of the season, knowing that His promised outcome will always come to pass in His perfect timing.

Unrequited Love

Did you hear the sentiment of unrequited love in Leah's second *because* statement? This phrase has formed the basis of countless books, poems, songs, and movies. Maybe you've been the victim of this feeling when your high school crush didn't respond with the same feelings you hoped they would. Psychologists define this hurtful experience as any love that isn't returned with matching intensity. It's clear that Leah lived in this paradigm for many years.

I've often wondered whether we treat God with similar contempt, by withholding His rightful praise during unfavourable circumstances?

In Luke 17:11–19, ten men afflicted with leprosy desperately pleaded with Jesus to heal them. This devastating disease not only killed the body over time but excluded each man from engaging in society, destroying them emotionally and relationally in the process. With compassion, Jesus lovingly responded by granting each a miraculous healing and reintegration into their families.

Interestingly their recovery came with a caveat. They needed to show themselves to the temple priests for a full bill of health. Luke 17:14 says that they were healed as they went, suggesting that the healing required a faith-filled and obedient action.

This principle is extremely important for us to remember in our own Christian journey.

These ten men were fully restored and reinstated into society. But only one, a foreigner, returned to Jesus with praise to acknowledge the healing encounter.

If we were God, with infinite knowledge of all things, and knew that ninety percent of our innate goodness would be squandered on people who simply resume their lives without a single thought of thanks for their healing, would we still grant their requests?

That's what Jesus did! Our concept of unrequited love has never been part of His vocabulary. His love, mercy, and blessing aren't contingent on our affirmation. We plainly read in 1 John 4:8 that *"God is love,"* and 1 Corinthians 13:4–7 elaborates on this to help us understand more fully the framework of His perpetual loving nature:

> Love is patient and kind. Love is not jealous or boastful or proud or rude. It does not demand its own way. It is not irritable, and it keeps no record of being wronged.

It does not rejoice about injustice but rejoices whenever the truth wins out. Love never gives up, never loses faith, is always hopeful, and endures through every circumstance. (NLT)

Likewise, our praise to Jehovah Jireh shouldn't be contingent on what He's given us. We are called to honour and celebrate Him for His eternal, unchanging character and limitless capability irrespective of the outcome. He offered us love and goodness while we were still stained with the ugliness of sin. When we had no way to appropriately reciprocate His inexpressible grace, He loved us. This is who He is and we have been created for relationship with Him.

In accepting His inexpressible gift of salvation, being privileged to stand as temples of praise, let's actively choose to imitate the one who *"came back to Jesus, shouting, 'Praise God!'"* (Luke 17:15, NLT). Let's offer daily gratitude and serve as a conduit of His selfless love to all people.

Heart Check

What is overflowing from your heart right now? Praise, concern, apathy, hope, truth? Are you willing to trust our faithful God in the storms of life when the waves crash, the wind blows, and the waters rise? As Christ-followers, we all have a unique and divine call on our lives that will be realized as we hold tightly to the dream God has planted in our hearts.

If the world has drowned out the still, soft voice of the Holy Spirit's call, it's time to intentionally amplify the sound of His voice. Remove the distractions, put down the phone, break away from the crowd, and invite the Lord's voice to echo in your heart again with this simple request: *"Speak, for your servant is listening"* (1 Samuel 3:10). You are called to greatness, though greatness often looks different from what our culture would call great. Jesus's recipe for success involves surrendering to godly servanthood and draping ourselves in humility to help the lost find His heart.

On my forty-seventh birthday, I took some time to practice this posture with intention. As the house became quiet, with everyone gone for work and school, I sat on our sun-drenched deck and said "Speak, Lord, for your servant is listening" before allowing space for the clatter of my daily thoughts to fall silent.

After some time, the Holy Spirit spoke several phrases that I'm actively living out to this day. He gently invited me to grow to love the place and people He had placed in my sphere of influence. He told me to check my heart and assess my motives through the lens of His loving heart. Finally, He advised me not to compare my growth with anyone else's, for we are all matured in His customized incubator designed just for us.

Honestly, I had to chew on these statements. My human nature balked at the implications. It sounded to me like God was asking me to play left field rather than thrive in the limelight.

But as I allowed this message to soak through the filter of His humility, the call aligned coherently with the words of famous preacher Charles Spurgeon, who posited,

> Is it not a curious thing that whenever God means to make a man great, He always first breaks him in pieces? ...That is His usual way of working! He makes you hungry before He feeds you! He strips you before He robes you! He makes nothing of you before He makes something of you![13]

Spurgeon used the examples of Jacob and David as examples of God's divine methodology for transformation, beginning with humility and thriving with praise to One who is worthy of everything.

Let's not be obsessed with our starting points or rate of progress. Rather, as the disciple John said, let's determine, *"He must become greater and greater, and I must become less and less"* (John 3:30, NLT). When we spend less time focusing on ourselves and more time listening to God's voice and magnifying the greatness of Yahweh through praise, we benefit

---

[13] Adrian Warnock, "God Breaks Those He Wants to Make Great," *Patheos*. October 18, 2009 (www.patheos.com/blogs/adrianwarnock/2009/10/god-breaks-those-he-wants-to-make-great/).

by savouring the journey and falling deeper in love with the Author of our destiny.

The Lord our God, who is from everlasting to everlasting, who stretched out the heavens and created the earth, and who gave life and breath to every living thing, knows your name, hears your heart, and loves you beyond our ability to fathom His heart. This is what the Spirit of the Lord said through the prophet Isaiah for the benefit of anyone who has their ears open to hear, *"for since the world began, no ear has heard and no eye has seen a God like you, who works for those who wait for him!"* (Isaiah 64:4, NLT) Just like Leah, the Lord hears you and loves you. He sees your heart and knows your mind.

While our enemy vehemently challenges these facts, I encourage you to stand firm on what you know to be true about God. Rehearse His faithful actions. Celebrate His unchanging character. Praise His glorious name. Choose to stay close to His heart and be intentional by opening your ears to hear His beautiful melody echoing over you. Remember the words of Zephaniah: *"The Lord your God is with you. He is a hero who saves you. He happily rejoices over you, renews you with his love, and celebrates over you with shouts of joy"* (Zephaniah 3:17, GW).

I invite you to pause and listen to His song of love before resolutely determining to praise Him in return.

Reflection Time

- God often uses our painful experiences to reach our distracted souls. What message has He spoken to you in times like this?

- Our God is big enough to hold our questions of lament, anger, and frustration as we express our raw emotions. Which of His promises speak of greater hope and purpose beyond your current challenges?

- Job 42:5 celebrates how Job relinquished the deity he thought he knew and praised the amazing realization of the God who truly is. What false assumptions do you need to surrender in order to praise the true transcendent nature of God?

- How might God be using your current trials, weakness, or pain to magnify His power while transforming your mess into His message of hope?

Leah's Third Son, Levi

(BECAUSE #3)

Again she conceived, and when she gave birth to a son she said, "Now at last my husband will become attached to me, because I have borne him three sons." So he was named Levi. (Genesis 29:34)

Some English words have a visceral feel to them. Maybe it's the phonetics that elicit a specific reaction, or an experiential association that heightens our emotions.

Think of a word like *bubble*. Try saying it fast, then slow. Emphasize the different syllables or change the tone to something more whimsical and you might find yourself smiling. Maybe you can associate this word with a fun memory of a bath or visit to a fair.

Conversely, there are words at the opposite end of the spectrum that can cause us to feel pain. Rejection is one such word. Its edges are sharp and angular. It can elicit imagery that pierces the heart with all-too-familiar barbs. This word conveys the act of throwing something away, or refusing to accept it. A medical connotation denotes the failure of an organ post-transplant, or the ejection of vomit from the body.

Try rereading the verse that begins this chapter and listen to Leah's heart cry of rejection. It punctuated the season she found herself in. She desperately hoped for a monumental change to transform her relationship with Jacob, rendering her far more than a dispensable object.

There is a paradigm called the pain cycle, which originates with a painful trigger point. This leads to an individual deploying a habitual coping mechanism, which in turn seems to provoke a false assumption that others will perpetually reject them.

For example, consider a person who feels overlooked. This can trigger in them a habitual flight response and culminates in them imagining they'll always be excluded from friendship circles.

The pain of rejection stings. It can rock us to our core and then kick us more when we're down. If this is you, please know that I hear you and believe that God will meet you in your pain with the steadfast knowledge of His peace and acceptance. Why? Because you mean so much more to Him than any earthly interaction could match.

Instead of allowing this pain-filled paradigm to perpetually imprison your heart, try substituting God's truth cycle.

For this same example, a person can regulate their feeling of rejection by declaring the truth behind the lie and choosing to behave differently, saying, "But I know that God says I am significant. As a result, I choose to be self-controlled."

Many could relate to Leah during this part of her journey. Genesis 29:34 tells us that she again conceived—which should be good news, right?—and gave birth to a son. Awesome! Three sons... what more could she ask for?

But then the verse reveals the sting in her heart: *"Now at last my husband will become attached to me, because I have borne him three sons."* Can you hear the pain behind these words? "After all I've done," she laments, "I hope my husband will finally love me. What else must I do to meet the longing of my heart?"

Leah named her third son Levi, which translates into Hebrew as "attached." Our protagonist's clear hope was somehow that this new arrival would cement a loving bond between her and Jacob.

LEAH'S THIRD SON, LEVI (BECAUSE #3)

God had now granted her three sons, but all Leah could fathom was a trilogy of despair. She was walking through life as a victim of her husband, her circumstances, and arguably her God.

Have you trudged somewhere similar, reliving the pain of yesterdays gone by? Are you obsessed with excavating past hurts instead of choosing a different path into the arms of your loving heavenly Father? He knows our pain yet wants to replace our shovel with a ladder so we can climb from despair's pit into the bright future He has prepared for us.

Anxiety and depression are enemies of the human condition and they don't discriminate on the basis of who you are, what you do, where you come from, your gender, your level of education, or your worldview. They can impede and stifle your ability to find pleasure, contentment, joy, peace, and happiness.

Russ Harris, author of *The Happiness Trap*, shares a staggering statistic: thirty percent of adults in the United States will suffer from a recognized psychological disorder during their lifetime. The World Health Organization was projecting that depression would become the second largest global challenge given its debilitating effects and multifaceted treatment. Russ adds that in any given week one in ten adults will suffer from clinical depression and one in five will face this at some time during their lives.[14]

While medications and psychological interventions can play an important role in rehabilitation, neither can address the arguably greater need in one's life: genuine affirmation and godly purpose, which can only be sourced from the Author of life. As God's Word says, *"Many are the plans in a person's heart, but it is the Lord's purpose that prevails"* (Proverbs 19:21).

By partnering with God's perfect plans and purpose, we experience meaningful fulfillment in labouring towards a divine goal powered by His everlasting strength, transcendent wisdom, and holy relationships.

STUCK TOGETHER LIKE GLUE

It's really interesting that Leah used the word "attachment."

John Bowlby, a twentieth-century British psychologist, psychiatrist, and psychoanalyst, spent his career pioneering the notion of *attachment theory*. He stated,

---

[14] Harris, *The Happiness Trap*, 3.

> Intimate attachments to other human beings are the hub around which a person's life revolves, not only when he is an infant or a toddler or a schoolchild but through his adolescence and his years of maturity and on into old age.[15]

Bowlby further added that we are malleable in our developmental psychology. So even problematic relational experiences can culminate in our potential to give love and reflect the freedom that flows from mature attachments.

Healthy relationships and attachments are foundational in God's design for us throughout our lives. Psalm 68:6 says that God *"places the lonely in families; he sets the prisoners free and gives them joy"* (NLT) and has designed the church community as a tangible representation of His familial love, acceptance, and help for every person.

The blessing of this design, however, hinges on following His guidelines in fostering healthy and life-giving relationships. If we don't attach together using godly principles, we run the risk of loving things and using people instead of loving people and using resources given for God's intended purpose.

That's exactly what was described in Romans 1:21, in which the apostle Paul wrote, *"They knew God but did not praise and thank him for being God. Instead, their thoughts were pointless, and their misguided minds were plunged into darkness"* (GW). By blaming God for our mismanagement of His good purpose, we absolve ourselves of our failed obligations. This isn't the Creator's fault. It is our responsibility to live with praise.

No wonder the Bible talks about our God-given responsibility to live counterculturally in the world for His good purpose, our fulfillment, and to the benefit of all. As Romans 12:1–2 says,

> And so, dear brothers and sisters, I plead with you to give your bodies to God because of all he has done for you. Let them be a living and holy sacrifice—the

---

[15] John Bowlby, *Attachment and Loss, Volume Three* (New York, NY: Basic Books, 1982), 442.

kind he will find acceptable. This is truly the way to worship him. Don't copy the behavior and customs of this world, but let God transform you into a new person by changing the way you think. Then you will learn to know God's will for you, which is good and pleasing and perfect. (NLT)

OUR MICROWAVE SPIRITUALITY

During our painful circumstances and dysfunctional attachments, God refines us. My counselling professor regularly echoed his personal refrain, encouraging us to "trust God's process" in all seasons of our lives. When we don't trust in His goodness, when we grow discouraged and question God's plan, we may feel conflict between our own strategized timeline and God's master plan.

Even when reading the Bible, we can fall for faulty perceptions that convince us that all these incredible stories of transformation happened overnight. Instant transformation is often the exception, not the rule. Patience, diligence, and consistency are hard skills to practice when we need them most, yet they are keys to achieving God's purpose. The fact remains, despite our sometimes childish doubts and demands, that God never lets go of us; He is forever in the business of restoring relationships, recrafting dreams, and renewing hope.

God empowers us with our own free will, meaning that we'll always have the choice to surrender and allow God to do what only He can do. Sometimes we petition God to change a person or a circumstance, but He responds with such disarming care, asking, "Dear child, are you willing to open up your hands and release that which is keeping you bound in order to take hold of the love, joy, peace patience, kindness, goodness, faithfulness, gentleness, and self-control I have for you in becoming My change agent in the world?"

When I reflect on a recent season when I had no answers for the challenges that lay ahead, I smile. The problems seemed monstrous, the relational disconnects next level. And my attitude required a lot of adjustment too! No doubt the hosts of heaven gave a little chuckle as I voiced words offering God untethered access, an open invitation to surrender which brought sincere joy to His heart. My juvenile demand sounded like this: "God, change my circumstances." Then, after a significant pause, I continued with an increasingly humble option: "And if not, then change my heart to live with what You have allowed."

There are no prizes for correctly guessing which requests God answered, resulting in a changed man with a transformed heart. This answer didn't come without sacrifice, tears, and much heartache, but over time His answer revealed itself as a perfect fit for my spiritual metamorphosis. I was required to surrender my plan to His sovereign will.

Dr. Samuel Hemby, a friend and professor of theology at Southeastern University, introduced me to the Change Triangle. This paradigm demonstrates that three heart postures are required before sustained change can occur:

1. Someone is hurting enough to initiate a change.
2. Someone is resourceful enough to identify potential change options.
3. Someone is resilient enough to sustain the desired change.

Given this lens, I wonder how well this would have worked for Leah's predicament. Had the hurt gone deep enough to make her search for a divine solution? Did she know God well enough to trust Him for His perfect solution? Was her resilience and support structure sufficient to allow for this sustained transformation?

I would encourage you to consider a current challenge in your own life and take inventory. How might you be positioned for God's transformation using this paradigm?

Without God's anchor of truth drawing our focus back to His purpose and promise, our feelings will rise and fall based on our subjective perspective.

Reading between the lines of Leah's story, Jacob didn't see, hear, or attach himself to her, but the Lord was perpetually available to fill the void left by her absent husband.

At times, we too may look for validation in all the wrong places to hopefully stabilize our own insecurities. But if we can pause long enough to control our fickle thoughts and confront our fears, we will hear God's gentle truth spoken to our hearts. In these moments, our true self can be heard, seen, known, and loved by our loving heavenly Father.

Listen carefully to God's tender words as He prophetically speaks over the wayward nation of Israel, as well as to us:

> But then I will win her back once again. I will lead her into the desert and speak tenderly to her there. I will return her vineyards to her and transform the Valley of Trouble into a gateway of hope. (Hosea 2:14–15, NLT)

Our heavenly Father comes to us, the prodigal, and tenderly says, "I will win you back with my abundant love and grace. I will do a restoration work in the dry and arid places of your heart, leading to My perpetual hope." His safe and secure attachment to you is ready and available whenever you are.

My Foggy Teacher

In life, peace and pain usually coexist. We might try to eliminate pain from our lives, believing that its absence will lead to perfect peace; however, there is no biblical evidence for this equation. Instead pain becomes a teacher that points us back to Jesus, the Prince of Peace who brings us comfort in the storm.

This lesson became abundantly clear to me during an experience while living in Jakarta, Indonesia during high school. One weekend, our family drove to visit friends in a remote town centrally located on the island of Java. Our friends took us on an unforgettable adventure to an extinct volcano. With so much opportunity for exploration paired with a little danger, what more could a teenage kid want?

Thirty minutes into an enthralling game of hide-and-seek on the volcano's immense crater floor, the atmosphere radically changed. Given the fluctuating climactic conditions, the stifling humidity ushered in a dense fog bank. The visibility was reduced to zero almost instantly. Panic set in fast given our isolated positions.

Anticipating our escalating fear, the host family took charge of the situation and shouted for everyone to stay still and remain calm as the phenomenon would soon pass. The presence of such oppressive fog lasted for about two minutes, though it felt like hours. While I couldn't see the others around me, their constant reassuring words offered peace and security amid chaos.

In his final encouragements to the church in Philippi, Paul gave us similar instructions about life's challenging seasons. Detailing a recipe to experience God's transcendent peace, he advises us to always be full of joy in the Lord and considerate of all, not to worry but pray (and praise) about everything and thank God for all He has done. Through this practice of gratitude, we will experience God's peace, a peace that exceeds our understanding and guards our hearts and minds in Jesus.

He shares one final thought: *"Fix your thoughts on what is true, and honorable, and right, and pure, and lovely, and admirable. Think about things that are excellent and worthy of praise"* (Philippians 4:8, NLT). Rehearsing and meditating on this wise counsel serves to strengthen our divine attachment and deepen our abiding connection with our heavenly Father.

Recordkeeping

I've found that maintaining a journal of my God-attachment experiences and the miracles He has performed helps when life's storms try to scream above the call to praise. Reflecting over these journal entries is so encouraging; they inspire praise, instill hope, and fuel my faith towards forward movement based on God's historical and trustworthy provisions. The practice of journalling keeps my heart in alignment with what God has called me to do.

Moses didn't have a journal to keep track of his own lived experiences of God's faithfulness. Instead he clung to a tangible testimony.

When God called him to lead Israel out of slavery, Moses raised several questions to release himself from the invitation. God wasn't asking

Moses to carry out this immense feat in his own ability, though. Like us, Moses was called to rely on God's power to achieve the task.

In proving this to Moses, God asked him a simple question: *"What is that in your hand?"* (Exodus 4:2, NLT) In a response reminiscent of Bible Jeopardy, I wonder whether Moses responded, "What is a staff for $200?"

No, God wasn't testing Moses's ability to identify a wooden object; He was highlighting a tangible symbol of His faithfulness, presence, and power for Moses and Israel. This everyday object would become a permanent sign of God's faithfulness as Moses accessed its symbolic power to part the Red Sea, create a gushing spring to quench the nation's thirst, and save the Israelites from the attacking Amalekites. That staff was a constant reminder of God's presence as the people walked the wilderness for four decades.

We can do the same today! What is in your heart and hand as a tangible reminder of God's presence? Maybe you could keep a verse written on a piece of paper in your wallet. Perhaps it's the Bible app on your phone, a picture hanging in your office, or the miracle child living in your house.

A key to living out God's promise for you is to be faithful with what He has given you as a personal sign of His powerful and abiding presence. With this symbol atop your mind and God's praise on your lips, confidently stand steadfast in the storm using His authority as you daily embody the testimony He has created you to be. Take hold of what's in your hand—in other words, the symbols which inspire praise to rise from your heart—and use these as sacred messages alongside God's Word.

Don't compare what you have to anyone else. Moses's staff wasn't for another; it was what God gave *him*. The same is true for you. So cling to the trophies of His presence and praise in ways that are authentically you for His glory and honour.

As Eugene Peterson poetically wrote, "Be just who you are—no more, no less. Pray prayers that gradually internalize a robust confidence in God's sovereignty and a relaxed acceptance of our humanity."[16] Be the

---

[16] Eugene H. Peterson, *Follow the Leader*. Regent College, Vancouver, Audio CD, 2000.

special person God has created you to be while praising the One who honours the lowly and gives His surpassing strength to the timid.

Is It Time Yet?

So have you got your "staff"? Are you standing side by side with Leah in the storm? Believing for things to change? Trusting God to perform the long-awaited miracle that's on the horizon? Still waiting?

Ah, yes. The timing part…

"Oh, I hear you," Leah would say with a wry smile. "We are called to be a faithful representative of what God has entrusted to us, and to stand resolutely while waiting on His perfect yet unknown timing."

When our kids were young, they would regularly ask when they could have a treat—or go swimming, watch a movie, or visit their grandparents… the list could go on. You get the idea. Sometimes the answer was "Right now." Other times it was "Later." Still other times we had something even better in mind, something their little minds couldn't even imagine.

But do you think they could understand this at the time? Kiboshing their requests rarely brought them much comfort. In fact, sometimes it heralded an epic meltdown. Yet over time they learnt to trust that something good might happen if they could just hold on.

Isn't the same true for us? After all, we're sometimes like kids dressed in adult clothes.

A pastor, friend, and mentor of mine once helped me navigate my own meltdown while wrestling with a God-given dream I'd held for several years earlier. After months of waiting for a breakthrough, nothing happened and I became very impatient.

With a mixture of frustration and anxiety, I called my godly friend, Kyle. His gentle response turned out to contain very wise counsel, even though it wasn't all that comforting in the moment.

"I feel like God's delay is actually His divine protection for you," he replied.

Kyle's discernment was profound, not to mention correct, but this godly counsel directly challenged my volatile human emotions. My preferred answer would have been: "It'll happen in three days. Or a year.

Or a decade. Just give me a definitive timeline so I can know when it's going to happen."

As I'm learning, though, God often doesn't work that way. He alone knows when we're ready to carry the increasing weight of His purpose in and through our lives for His glory. He won't be rushed, manipulated, or coerced into doing anything early, despite our whining. His perfect plan is attached to His perfect timing.

Soon after receiving Kyle's message, I was reading Moses's life story when I found my attention drawn by a few key verses. God was delivering the Ten Commandments to Moses at Mount Sinai, instructing Israel on godly living and future enemy encounters. He then included a curious caveat:

> But I will not drive them [our enemies] out in a single year, because the land would become desolate and the wild animals too numerous for you. Little by little I will drive them out before you, until you have increased enough to take possession of the land. (Exodus 23:29–30)

Take a moment to reread these two verses—slowly. What parts stand out to you? Is it the timestamps associated with the promise? It was for me.

God says that this victory won't happen in a single year. It will instead happen little by little!

"Ah, excuse me, God, but that's not an exact date. It's an indefinite timeline. I'd prefer the verse to read that it will happen with lightning speed, that You'll get me to the destination within six months… more than a year? That sounds ridiculously slow."

While watching a construction program on television, I learned that, in pouring concrete, the slower it dries, the stronger it becomes. With a super-fast curing comes the increased likelihood of a brittle and compromised structure, despite a strong outward appearance. A slower process leads to robust structural integrity, even though the wait can feel onerous.

Using this lens, consider God's rationale for the indefinite timestamp: the land would become desolate, the wild animals would be too numerous, and the people would need to increase in number and character to possess the land with God's wisdom and tenacity.

The same is true for us. Devoid of our fortitude to praise God in the storm and hold relentlessly to His perfect plan and timing, our haphazard emotions cause us to be eaten alive by fear and anxiety; we exist aimlessly and live far beneath our divine calling.

In other words, God loves us far too much to give us this assignment before we're ready.

So with a deep breath and intentional resolve, I decided to consider how this would play out in my own life. If God went through and wiped out all my fears and concerns right now and instantly granted everything He had promised me, could I sustain it all? Moreover, would I have the maturity to thrive? Likely not.

This is potentially why God, with His all-surpassing wisdom, doesn't grant such requests before His appointed time.

In Philippians 1:6, Paul confidently boasts, *"And I am certain that God, who began the good work within you, will continue his work until it is finally finished on the day when Christ Jesus returns"* (NLT). God is completely trustworthy, so our invitation to ongoing spiritual development comes by way of praise plus faith/trust plus surrender plus patience.

Like King David, who developed his godly dependence and intimate relationship with his Father through praise, worship, and prayer over many seasons, let's position ourselves securely in God's gentle hands by saying, "Lord, thank You for the unique process You have me in. You are constantly growing me, teaching me, and refining me until the incremental stages of Your perfection in me are complete. Thank You for protecting me and everyone around me until Your work in me is complete. I trust You and patiently surrender to Your loving heart in developing the roots of my life until they can hold the weight of Your call. In the waiting, I will choose to praise You before, during, and after Your answers through me are fulfilled."

I wonder if Leah had a similar prayer in mind as she closed the book on her third son, Levi. I'm guessing that she must have! The evidence is undeniable, although there are no specific revelations as to what happened between the verses of Genesis 29:34–35 to detail the incredible transformation that was coming.

As we walk forward with this young lady, pregnant with God's potential, we will see her divine metamorphosis firsthand. Please keep this truth in mind—that whatever God does for one, He has in His heart and power to do for anyone who is willing.

This time, in this space, I choose to attach myself to You, God, praising You for Your limitless ability as Creator, Healer, and Restorer.

Reflection Time

- How much of your disappointment is rooted in the unrealistic expectations that a flawed human will love you perfectly?

- In seasons of hurt, your prayer might be for God to change your circumstances, yet God's divine plan is that prayer changes us. What do you need to lay down for God to change you?

- In Hosea 2:14–15, God reveals His plan to win Israel back with words of love spoken in the desert. Take a moment to personalize this invitation and imagine these dry and arid places as His masterful workshop of hope for you.

- A specific timeline can create tunnel vision for our mental priorities. Yet our invitation to praise comes in a liminal season of discomfort and stretching. Which name for God is most important for knowing Him better during this season?

Leah's Fourth Son, Judah

She conceived again, and when she gave birth to a son she said, "This time I will praise the Lord." So she named him Judah. Then she stopped having children. (Genesis 29:35)

Acclaimed American poet, author, screenwriter, actor, and civil rights activist Maya Angelou once wrote, "We delight in the beauty of the butterfly but rarely admit the changes it has gone through to achieve that beauty."[17] What truth!

Have you ever longingly aspired to become a world-changer, elite athlete, or art prodigy without wanting to make the huge sacrifices necessary to reach that pinnacle? Each time the Olympic Games occur, I often catch myself considering the cost of the athletes' pursuit.

Similarly, a caterpillar's metamorphosis into a phenomenal winged wonder demands all-encompassing buy-in. The resultant butterfly was originally birthed from an egg as a caterpillar. It then consumes a huge quantity of food before spinning its chrysalis of transformation. In that chrysalis, the exoskeleton dissolves into a soup-like consistency

---

[17] Maya Angelou, *Rainbow in the Cloud: The Wisdom and Spirit of Maya Angelou* (New York, NY: Random House, 2014).

during cellular regeneration and emerges with the amazing ability to fly.

Apologies to anyone who may be eating while reading this graphic description!

Some would suggest that the cocoon represents a resting phase for this soon-to-appear majestic creation, but nothing could be further from the truth. Continuous and uncomfortable changes are always at work to herald this transformation's awe-inspiring climax.

Human pregnancy holds some similar principles. The intense nine-month gestational period affects all manner of hormones in the mother's body, resulting in new life.

I wonder whether this was true for Leah. While the Bible doesn't elaborate on any specific changes that occur between her first and fourth pregnancies, her progressive metamorphosis was multifaceted and the spiritual transformation undeniable.

Remember Leah's life before her spiritual chrysalis. She was weak-eyed, unwanted, and unloved. Before birthing Reuben, she was denied affection. "God's seen my misery. Surely Jacob will love me now." Then came Simeon. "The Lord heard that I'm unloved, so here is His compensatory gift." Then came Levi. "Finally Jacob will lovingly attach to me, based on the male lineage I've produced for him."

If only there had been a spiritual camera to trace the real-time changes in her heart as God's revolutionary metamorphosis occurred. She deconstructed old beliefs, challenged previously held pain, and surrendered the past for a globally impacting future.

As Genesis 29:35 reads, *"She conceived again, and when she gave birth to a son she said, 'This time I will praise the Lord.' So she named him Judah."*

Did Leah know something special about this boy in advance? Could this have led to her about-face? Did she have any idea that the Messiah of the world would be born several generations later, springing forth from this very lineage?

This is all curious speculation, but what can we see and hear for certain? This time, she didn't name her son according to any multifaceted afflictions, difficult circumstances, or longing for her husband's affection. Instead Leah chose to bestow on her fourth son the name Judah, meaning "praise."

Some commentaries have Leah uttering an exuberant statement, *Soli Deo Gloria*, which translates to "I will praise the Lord"—or *Yahuwdah*, which means "May God be praised!" Either way, even before this fresh revelation of God's goodness, Leah resolved to praise Him more than ever.

In the 2015 movie *War Room*, written by Alex and Stephen Kendrick, the character of Miss Clara shares many discipleship principles with her mentee, Elizabeth. One of the biblical gems shared during these coaching sessions goes like this: "To win the fight, you've got to have the right strategy and the right resources, because victories don't come by accident."[18]

There are no accidental victories in marriage, life, or spiritual maturation. But with one's heart posture continually surrendered to God's praise and purpose, we can stand back and watch what He will do. This was a posture diametrically opposed to how Leah had historically responded when things didn't go her way, when life was unfair without reason. Even when her circumstances didn't change within a few days, she chose to elevate her focus to praise God above all.

Leah's life speaks profoundly to the importance of making this godly choice. She made the decision to be better instead of bitter, look heavenward instead of casting her eyes down at the dirt, and move forward with God-inspired tenacity.

Having declared resentment, apathy, and bitterness in naming her first three sons, Leah drew a line in the sand and decided to praise the Lord of all creation for who He was as opposed to living perpetually as a circumstantial victim. What a celebrated testimony of divine transformation!

THE CHOICE IS MADE

Praise is an intentional choice to rehearse the truth of God's character and elevate His eternal promises above the malaise of our own reality. The Bible contains numerous examples of this.

---

[18] *War Room*, directed by Alex Kendrick (Los Angeles, CA: Sony, 2015).

In Psalm 69:30, King David, a descendant of Judah, penned a message to the sovereign Lord when he was overwhelmed by trouble and earnestly begged God to create a pathway through. Yet toward the end of the psalm, he radically adjusted his heart posture and burst forth in humble adoration, saying, *"I want to praise God's name with a song. I want to praise his great name with a song of thanksgiving"* (GW).

Likewise, the apostle Paul, instrumental in germinating the first Christian congregation in the city of Philippi, sat chained to a Roman soldier while awaiting execution. He penned his gratitude for God every time the Holy Spirit brought this thriving, faith-filled community to mind (Philippians 1:1–3).

Following two years of imprisonment, he lifted a heart full of praise to the God who had given him more than he could ever repay, a relationship more intimate than breathing and one that was much closer than the oppressor beside him. A person could easily grow embittered in such challenging circumstances, but ultimately Paul remained anchored to God's unshakable praise and purpose. His choices paved the way for generations of divine transformations to follow.

Praise becomes an attitudinal shift that inspires a person towards honouring God in all circumstances—that means when things are convenient or difficult, comfortable or hurtful, projected or unexpected, celebratory or frightening, painful or edifying. Not everything that happens in our lives will feel good or easy, but we serve a God in whom *all things* are divinely woven together for the holistic good of those who love God and actively surrender to His purpose. The Message translation puts it this way: *"That's why we can be so sure that every detail in our lives of love for God is worked into something good"* (Romans 8:28, MSG).

We must make a daily choice to surrender, and this choice aligns cohesively with Paul's statement in 1 Thessalonians 5:18 which beckons Christ-followers to *"in every situation [no matter what the circumstances] be thankful and continually give thanks to God; for this is the will of God for you in Christ Jesus"* (AMP).

In every season, the King of the universe and Lord of our hearts deserves our highest praise. He is in complete control 24/7 and worthy of everything, so let us celebrate together with Leah and offer God our sacrifice of praise both on the pinnacle of joy and in the valley of tears.

Changing the Present and Future

For Leah, her fourth son Judah became a metaphorical line in the sand. No, she couldn't go back and undo the dilapidated sandcastle of past mistakes. Neither could she foresee what was ahead. But she accepted the divine invitation to start from where she was now and daily change the ending through sustained godly action.

Listen to Leah declare her decision: "From this moment on, I'm choosing You, God, above my circumstances. My perspective is going to be different based on Your truth and anchored in the bedrock of solid faith with Jehovah Adonai as my Lord of Lords." Healing had found her in the desert of despair.

And the same healing is available for you today. Reach out. Don't squander God's praise by remaining in death's valley. He will rescue you. Our broken alleluia of surrender will be transformed into a song of triumph when placed in the hands of the Redeemer and Restorer.

Maybe you're at the stage where you want to commit to praise as a lifestyle but aren't quite sure where to begin.

Well, here is one option. Pastor Chris Hodges has created a set of personalized declarations that he uses in his daily devotions. Passionately rehearsed each day, these statements focus on the new identity Christ has formed within us. They remind us of this high calling. I would encourage you to begin by saying these each morning.

There are twelve declarations in Hodges's book, but here are six of them, slightly paraphrased.[19]

- Jesus is the Lord of my life, and I exist to praise and serve Him. I am growing closer to Him, and He is giving me His own anointing, blessing, influence and protection.
- Today, I give You my words, thoughts, actions and imagination and make them obedient to Jesus' authority in my life.

---

[19] The full list of declarations can be found at: Hodges, *Out of the Cave*, 89–90.

- I am disciplined, Christ in me is stronger than the evil desires that war against me. I wake up with praise, purpose, direction, and meaning every day of my life.
- I am called to reach people far from God and lead them on a spiritual journey to know Him, find freedom, discover purpose and make a difference.
- I bring my best self today. Through the power of Jesus name, the world will be better today because I served Him wholeheartedly.
- Today, I love God, love people, pursue excellence and choose joy. In every moment, I will praise my Lord and my God.

Personalizing Leah's confession—*"This time I will praise the Lord"* (Genesis 29:35)—is a test of our own integrity in wholeheartedly actioning God's faith-filled promises.

For example, when God told Noah in Genesis to build an ark so he and his family would be delivered from the global flood, he did so based on the faithful outcome God had already promised. In 1 Samuel, when God told Hannah that He was going to answer her prolonged prayer for a son, she stopped weeping, went home, and expected a child—which happened according to God's timing.

Holding confidently to God's Word with tenacious personal conviction sustained through praise shapes our prayers and desires as we choose to live by faith and not by sight.

In faith, Leah made a sincere confession toward godly action, naming her son Judah and thus praising the Lord for His sovereignty. Even if her husband wasn't in love with her, she chose to praise God for His goodness.

God is worthy of everything. In His great love and mercy, He chooses to lavish the blessing of His eternal presence on anyone who confesses Jesus as Lord. Amid His greatness, He created you, gifted you, and graced you to bring Him praise by aligning our calling with His perspective.

We have all been born with God-given potential to be His light and life in the world. As the omniscient and omnipotent Creator, He looks at you and sees every potential and wants to help you become all that He crafted you to be.

Given the vast limitations of our earthly language, Psalm 103:2–5 seeks to describe the awesomeness of God:

> Praise the Lord, my soul, and forget not all his benefits—who forgives all your sins and heals all your diseases, who redeems your life from the pit and crowns you with love and compassion, who satisfies your desires with good things so that your youth is renewed like the eagle's.

This is our God. The choice to praise is within our heart and mouth.

THE THIEF OF PRAISE

The enemy of our soul is forever seeking to steal praise from its rightful owner. In Ezekiel and Isaiah, God described Satan, a name which translates to Lucifer in Hebrew, as holding a prominent position in heaven before he greedily pursued equality with his Creator. This is what the sovereign Lord says:

> You were anointed as a guardian cherub, for so I ordained you. You were on the holy mount of God; you walked among the fiery stones. You were blameless in your ways from the day you were created till wickedness was found in you. (Ezekiel 28:14–15)

> How you have fallen from heaven, morning star, son of the dawn! You have been cast down to the earth, you who once laid low the nations! You said in your heart, "I will ascend to the heavens; I will raise my throne above the stars of God; I will sit enthroned on the mount of assembly, on the utmost heights of Mount

Zaphon. I will ascend above the tops of the clouds; I will make myself like the Most High." But you are brought down to the realm of the dead, to the depths of the pit. (Isaiah 14:12–15)

Despite the ironclad fact that Satan will never triumph over the Lord Most High, he still tried to coerce the praise and worship of Jesus during the desert temptation. In Matthew's gospel account, Jesus had just been baptized by John in the Jordan River and was led by the Holy Spirit into the desert. After two unsuccessful attempts to separate God's Son from complete reliance on His Father, Satan launched his final salvo.

> Again, the devil took him to a very high mountain and showed him all the kingdoms of the world and their splendor. "All this I will give you," he said, "if you will bow down and worship [praise] me."
>
> Jesus said to him, "Away from me, Satan! For it is written: 'Worship [praise] the Lord your God, and serve him only.'" (Matthew 4:8–11)

Engaging in praise and worship is about relating to God with an accurate picture of who He is. This is exactly what Jesus did in attesting that God is the only One worthy of all we can offer. Even though the manifestation of our praise may at times look different in various seasons of life, our primary objective and focus remain steadfast. For example, in grief you may be hurting so much that a song is almost impossible to muster, but you choose to come to God in your tearful brokenness since you can always trust Him more than your raw emotions of hurt, loss, and confusion.

During seasons of failure or disappointment, don't allow the enemy to harass or entrap you based on past sins that have already been forgiven. The precious blood of Jesus was freely given on the cross for all humanity. Everything was, and is, forgiven. God harbours no bitterness towards us and instead graciously exhorts us to live in His freedom. So don't allow the devil any license to hold you a victim; God's limitless grace is already signed, sealed, and delivered through the person of Jesus. Shame has no hold over you—and upon your confession of faith, you forever belong to our loving heavenly Father.

As Leah would testify, hurt and heartache brought her to the end of herself. But instead of it resulting in defeat, praise created an entryway for her into God's throne room of grace and victory.

On our knees, the purest praise can rise from our broken hearts and faltering lips as we celebrate our God, who is so close to the broken-hearted. Though we may not tangibly feel His perfect presence given the persistent jab of our pain, His arms gently enfold our deepest sorrows and steadily move us towards His greatest victories.

In his devotional, *Emotionally Healthy Spirituality, Day by Day*, pastor and author Peter Scazzero cites the prayer of an unknown Confederate soldier. This prayer is another heartfelt cry of praise to our God amid trying circumstances:

> I asked God for strength that I might achieve,
> I was made weak that I might learn to obey.
> I asked for health that I might do great things.
> I was given infirmity that I might do better things.
> I asked for riches that I might be happy;
> I was given poverty that I might be wise.
> I asked for power when I was young that I might hear the praise of men;
> I was given weakness that I might feel the need for God.
> I asked for all things that I might enjoy life;
> I was given life that I might enjoy all things.
> Almost despite myself, my unspoken prayers were answered.
> I am, among all people, most richly blessed.[20]

---

[20] Peter Scazzero, *Emotionally Healthy Spirituality, Day by Day* (Grand Rapids, MI: Zondervan, 2014), 95.

This kind of godly humility also invites praise to exude from our hearts. The apostle Paul likewise alluded to this in demonstrating how a painful challenge brought him to a glorious conclusion:

> …so I wouldn't get a big head, I was given the gift of a handicap to keep me in constant touch with my limitations. Satan's angel did his best to get me down; what he in fact did was push me to my knees. No danger then of walking around high and mighty! At first I didn't think of it as a gift, and begged God to remove it. Three times I did that, and then he told me, "My grace is enough; it's all you need. My strength comes into its own in your weakness."
>
> Once I heard that, I was glad to let it happen. I quit focusing on the handicap and began appreciating the gift. It was a case of Christ's strength moving in on my weakness. Now I take limitations in stride, and with good cheer, these limitations that cut me down to size—abuse, accidents, opposition, bad breaks. I just let Christ take over! And so the weaker I get, the stronger I become. (2 Corinthians 12:7–10, MSG)

Purpose in the Waiting

Kristy and I waited a long eighteen months for confirmation that we were pregnant. Each month that passed without a positive result was incredibly heartbreaking. When unsuspecting friends asked when we were planning to start a family, the figurative blade sank that much deeper into our hearts.

During my own devotional times, the Lord challenged me to make an intentional choice to praise Him for His perfect plan and timing. Initially, it wasn't easy. I started thinking like Abram, saying, "How can I honour you when we still don't have what we hope for?"

At the time, I was a worship leader at our church in Brisbane and the tension of these opposing forces became impossible to hold. There were days where I journalled with more pleas than heartfelt confessions.

Sometimes I just sat in silence, listening to praise music to bolster my fluctuating faith.

During this waiting season, we registered to attend the 2004 Hillsong conference in Sydney. I suspected this would be a fertile time of corporate praise to God with thousands of global delegates. While benefiting greatly from the conference's teaching, I began rehearsing my own invitation to praise more consistently and passionately. While doing so, the divine image of a rainbow dropped into my spirit.

Almost a decade earlier, I had written a personal praise song called "Rainbows," testifying to a miracle I'd experienced during a missions trip. The lyrics now elicited even greater significance. The rainbow imagery testified to God's faithfulness to Noah and his family while stirring inspiration to create a praise event at our home church.

I couldn't wait to return home and develop this idea with Andrew, a pastor, friend, and our church's creative director. The event would serve as an indelible reminder of God's faithfulness, just as the rainbow was for Noah. Developing this praise experience caused my heart to soar despite our childless reality. Psalm 119:108 became my constant refrain: *"Accept, Lord, the willing praise of my mouth, and teach me your laws."*

As my practiced discipline became praise, our planning for the event gained momentum. Throughout all this, little did Kristy and I suspect that the Lord was working beyond our knowledge to perform two microscopic miracles in Kristy's womb.

Eight months after this transformative night of praise, we celebrated God's manifest goodness in holding our twins, Sierra and Cody.

Even though our paths can sometimes be dark and difficult, our dreams stretched far beyond our limits of comfort, praise changed our focus. Instead of dwelling on the idol of having children, we chose to honour His name. In that transition, God birthed a revelation in our hearts, a renewal in our spirits, and placed two precious miracles in our arms.

The comedic side of the story is that, unbeknownst to me, Kristy had been praying and trusting God for a multiple birth situation, since she didn't want to have to endure this hugely emotional process a second time. So during our emergency ultrasound, which happened around week eight of pregnancy under some traumatic circumstances, the obstetrician's revelation of two heartbeats came as no surprise to her.

For me? Well, that's a different story. Kristy says that I adopted a foetal position. I couldn't comprehend how we were going to manage two kids simultaneously. But in hindsight, I am so incredibly thankful for how everything turned out.

After composing myself mentally and emotionally, I initiated a polite conversation with her and requested that moving forward we work diligently on our communication skills and prayer alignment.

She just smiled and held up two fingers. I love her so much.

My mum has shared her perspective on our journey in her own inspirational autobiography, *Unleashing Courageous Faith*.[21] We are so thankful for our parents' support and prayers during this season.

Word by Word

I would love to have stood with Leah as she uttered that epic phrase, "This time I will praise the Lord," with heartfelt intentionality. Each word was spoken with holy decisiveness to underscore her resolution.

This godly affidavit is a hope-filled invitation for every successive generation, heralding the person of our praise, Jesus, as is poetically described in John's gospel: *"So the Word became human and made his home among us"* (John 1:14, NLT).

I invite you to practice speaking Leah's confession slowly and deliberately with me: "This time I will praise the Lord."

Let's take a moment to break it down. Or rap it out! Whichever works for you.

"This time" means now, in this moment, in this decision, at this fork in the road where we can choose either faith or fear. Her declaration wasn't reliant on what had happened yesterday. This starts right now, in the present moment, and will continue on into the future.

"I" is a reminder that this is a choice we make unilaterally. It doesn't matter what those around you are doing, thinking, or saying. You can make a decision that affects how you choose to see and honour God,

---

[21] Lynn Abrahams, *Unleashing Courageous Faith* (Croydon, AU: Green Hill Publishing, 2022).

giving Him praise befitting His character. You may be young or old, married or single, rich or poor, living in the city or the country... it really doesn't matter. You have a personal invitation and need to decide what to do with it.

"Will" indicates an inevitable outcome. As Leah verbalized this, she was very intentional in her choice of words. Notice that she didn't say *may*, *might*, or *could*. Her statement was pregnant with God-centric defiance. Despite her previous posture, despite what had or hadn't yet happened, this was her redefined stance in honouring God.

"Praise" has various synonyms, including expressions of respect and gratitude, honouring and glorifying, revering, adoring, exalting, ascribing, attributing, and giving one's devotion. But these barely scratch the surface unless God is made the benefactor of our praise.

"The Lord" then takes centre stage as the focal point of our adoration. When this happens, everything else becomes insignificant. Again, this is a choice. Worldly distractions scream for us to give praise to everything and anything but the name of Jesus, yet He alone is worthy of all praise and honour in every generation both now and forever throughout eternity.

The Bible records many similar statements from men and women who have emulated a similar lived trajectory. For example, Joshua and Caleb, as they returned to the Israelite nation and gave their report about overthrowing the city of Jericho. This courageous duo asserted, *"We should go up and take possession of the land, for we can certainly do it [with God's help]"* (Numbers 13:30). To put Caleb's statement in a different form: "This time we will follow the Lord."

Think back to Jesus's human mother, Mary. Stunned by the news that she, a virgin, would be divinely impregnated and give birth to the Messiah, she declared, *"I am the Lord's servant. May everything you have said about me come true"* (Luke 1:38, NLT). This could be rephrased, "This time I will submit to the Lord."

In both instances, these people decided to blaze a praise pathway into God's certain future. Could they clearly see to the other side before making these faith statements? No way. Were there some large obstacles in the way? You bet there were! But did they know their God and intentionally place praise-filled faith in Him above any conflicting voice in apprehending their God-determined future? Most definitely!

Paul's words to the church in Thessalonica add weight to these holy declarations. This man began life as a Christian hater and zealously persecuted the fledgling church of Jesus Christ, but his life was radically transformed by the power of God's grace. Paul's experience led him to embody this life-giving statement: *"Rejoice always, pray continually, give thanks [and praise] in all circumstances; for this is God's will for you in Christ Jesus"* (1 Thessalonians 5:16–18).

This Christian brother knew what it was like to be the persecutor. He then became the persecuted and was martyred for the sake of honouring his Saviour for the praise of Jesus's name. Paul demonstrated that our circumstances should not determine the level of our joy, the consistency of our prayers, the abundance of our thanks, or the quantity or persistence of our praise.

Friends, the choice is ours. Yet when we compare all that God has done for us, the love poured out in the person of Jesus, and the Holy Spirit given to empower us as His example to a lost world, praise begs to be released from the depths of who we are. Let's choose to join with all creation in celebrating the unfathomable goodness of our triune God, who is forever worthy of praise.

LIFE IN THE FAST LANE

We live in a busy world. Its endless refrain is to push harder, run faster, and achieve more than yesterday or risk being left behind. With the heaviness of our daily responsibilities, we can find ourselves losing connection with the present moment. Praise can easily become deprioritized.

Mindfulness is a hot-button term for meditation. Pop psychology describes mindfulness as the practice of purposely focusing one's attention on the present moment and accepting it without judgment. According to a Harvard study, mindfulness is being celebrated for stress reduction, physical health benefits, improved cognitive functioning, and increased life satisfaction.[22]

---

[22] Harvard Health, "Benefits of Mindfulness," *HelpGuide.org*. August 30, 2024 (www.helpguide.org/harvard/benefits-of-mindfulness.htm).

It's funny how God already knew this when He created us and instituted mindfulness as a rhythm to combat our life-depleting habits—by focusing on His goodness through praise. The psalmist knew this too and gave an invitation to follow this life-elevating path: *"My eyes stay open through the watches of the night, that I may meditate on your promises"* (Psalm 119:148).

I invite you right now to take a moment to slow down. Put down the book and just praise your Father God and Saviour Jesus for who they are. Ask the Holy Spirit to help you bring to mind the unchanging nature of God's character and recall how His power and grace have sustained you in seasons past. Maybe you want to play a song of praise, either to sing or just allow the words to wash over you as a fragrant praise offering.

Or maybe follow the example of my friend and mentor Michael W. Smith, the chief operating officer of the Association of Related Churches, who starts his day (1) giving praise and gratitude to Jesus, (2) remembering that we are His daily works-in-progress, constantly being renewed by the Holy Spirit, (3) and offering thanks to Jesus for calling us His friends (John 15:14–15).

Why not set a reminder on your phone and begin with a one-week test drive of doing this before objectively assessing the impact of this God-honouring daily restart?

I also encourage you to consider practically applying Leah's praise invitation through the Sixty Sixty Soul Revolution app challenge. Developed by the Gateway church in Austin, the app sends you a reminder every hour between 8:00 a.m. to 8:00 p.m. for sixty days to help foster a godly habit of praise amid our hectic schedules.

I get it! I often become so consumed with my own challenges and commitments that, despite my best intentions, I forget to give God the praise He continually deserves. So I'm grateful for resources like these that help us develop such praise rhythms in our daily lives.

A Jarring Halt

I used to hate rollercoasters. As a kid, I was the one who held up the line by sheepishly making a very awkward exit past the long line of cued patrons when my temporarily summoned courage rapidly melted into abject fear.

Thankfully, at the age of twelve, this fear morphed from terror into sheer elation. I successfully completed my inaugural ride and enjoyed the thrill of speed, weightlessness, twists, drops, banking curves, inversions, and corkscrews.

Sadly, these amazing sensations only last for a few minutes before everything comes to a halt with the shrill of brakes grinding against the metallic grates. Every rider's chest is momentarily pinned against their safety harness.

This is what it feels like in the second half of Genesis 29:35. Leah made her confession of praise, prophetically naming her son Judah. And then came these words: *"Then she stopped having children."* Why? What happened?

Well, I don't have a good explanation. I've done some research, but the Scriptures are silent as to the reasons. Commentators all have their own opinions on the matter. One theory says that Leah became infertile for a time. Another suggests, given the escalating jealousy of Jacob's other wife Rachel, that he stopped sleeping with Leah.

Both hypotheses are feasible, but they beg the question: what happened next?

This is a very relatable situation for many. We come off the high mountain of praise and find ourselves in a pit of despair. I know I have.

After enjoying a fun family vacation, we returned home only for me to have a meltdown with our kids in a way they certainly didn't deserve. (Sorry again, Cody and Sierra!) We went from the heights of fun and unity to a fragmented mess on the floor. Our children were so very gracious in forgiving me for behaving like a first-grade jerk. Afterward, praise was hard to honour in my guilt-ridden state. All I could muster was a humble apology and a broken alleluia.

What happens in you when you make a commitment to praise but then your world goes dark and you're lost in a maze of confusion? Whatever our reaction, one thing is for certain: our mess is no barrier to God's arms of grace.

Leah stands as a compelling testimony of this reality. In the next chapter, her story will continue in tandem with ours. Even as life ebbs and flows, I will choose to praise the Lord on the mountaintop of elation as well as in the valley of tears.

Reflection Time

- How have you experienced God's metamorphosis towards praise in your own journey?

- In Psalm 34:1 David says, *"I will praise the Lord at all times"* (NLT). This means praising God because He *is* good, not necessarily because we *feel* good. How often are you led by feelings versus the intentional choice to praise?

- Satan, the praise thief, is forever seeking to victimize us and steal what rightly honours God. Take some time now to denounce any hold he has over your heart and mind and make your own holy declaration to praise the Lord in this season.

- Try writing a set of declarations, or download the Sixty Sixty Soul Revolution app, and choose to rehearse these each morning for the next week. Note the changes you experience.

6

Praise Has Bad Days,
BUT PRAISE SEES THE END

> *When our lowest lows come on the heels of our highest highs, we feel confused, untethered and disorientated by the descent.*[23]
> —Chris Hodges

As I write, it is July 2022 and the pandemic is mostly behind us, although it still attracts some media attention after having ravaged the globe for eighteen long months. I celebrated with many others, both locally and globally, when vaccines became available for those who chose to take them.

However, a new dilemma emerged in due time. It became apparent that this vaccination did not translate to complete immunity. Breakthrough cases of COVID-19 were reported with increasing frequency. Therefore, despite doing everything humanly possible to protect oneself, including taking multiple doses of the so-called "wonder drug," it still wasn't enough.

While this example may not directly represent your lived experience, the fact remains: a depressed spiritual state is probable following a mountaintop experience with God. As Pastor Chris Hodges writes,

---

[23] Hodges, *Out of the Cave*, 107.

Depression often comes on the heels of a spiritual and emotional high. When we reach a milestone, attain a goal, or receive God's long-awaited answer to our prayers, we experience exhilaration, excitement and joy. But we can only sustain this level of high-octane energy for so long, and then our emotions have nowhere to go but down.[24]

How do your past experiences align with this? Perhaps you have an amazing weekend experiencing God in a variety of ways only for it all to dissolve as a Monday deadline hits. You celebrate an A on one exam only to feel the pressure of trying to maintain that success. You overcome a formidable health hurdle only to face a new diagnosis and barrage of treatment that's even more gruelling than what came before.

Leah was granted four tangible blessings from God, but now her inability to procreate combined with an ominous sisterly feud. The result? A downward spiral in the relationship between Jacob, Rachel, and Leah. It sounds like a soap opera.

The first salvo was fired by Rachel, whose envy over Leah's children escalated towards self-harm. She then gave Jacob a shocking ultimatum, saying, *"Give me children, or I'll die!"* (Genesis 30:1) And the award for Best Overdramatization of a Challenging Life Circumstance goes to…

While jealousy isn't listed among the seven deadly sins, mix together greed, wrath, and envy and you will very likely arrive at this endpoint.

Let's add some context to this plot and identify how praise fits into the landscape. As noted earlier, male heirs were considered a sign of godly favour while infertility was regarded as a curse. So Rachel found herself as a target, despite Jacob's devoted support. He could do nothing to improve this predicament, as acknowledged in his response to her: *"Am I God? …He's the one who has kept you from having children!"* (Genesis 30:2, NLT)

So, as per the culture at that time, Rachel gave her maidservant Bilhah to Jacob to act as a surrogate mother. The goal was to build a lineage, and this action succeeded in producing two sons for Jacob. The first was

---

[24] Ibid., 10.

named Dan, meaning *"God has vindicated me; he has listened to my plea and given me a son"* (Genesis 30:6), and the second Naphtali, meaning *"I have had a great struggle with my sister, and I have won"* (Genesis 30:8). No passive aggressive family dynamics there, right?

Retaliatory strikes seem like this family's love language. Leah jumped on the anger train and threw her maidservant Zilpah at Jacob to increase her own matriarchal footprint. This resulted in two more sons for Leah, including Gad, which translates to *"What good fortune!"* (Genesis 30:11), and Asher, which translates to *"How happy I am! The women will call me happy"* (Genesis 30:13).

It's so easy to critique Leah and ask what happened to her passionate declaration that this time she would praise the Lord. But then when the chips are down, you retreat towards a habitual behavioural pattern and seemingly forget God's goodness.

We may need to take a look in the mirror and ask for His eyes of grace to see our own mistakes.

But Leah's praise statement is so foundational for the Christian. It anchors us to the very heart of our Creator, Redeemer, and everlasting Source amidst our own challenges. We need His perspective to wisely navigate these pitfalls.

Knowing the challenges ahead, Jesus promised us a counsellor and comforter: *"And I will ask the Father, and he will give you another Advocate, who will never leave you. He is the Holy Spirit, who leads into all truth"* (John 14:16–17, NLT).

In an enlightening message I heard decades ago, Pastor Wayne Alcorn, national president of the Australian Christian Churches, uttered a profound phrase that resonated strongly in my heart. Wayne's father was a pastor and had received a vision that his son would follow in his footsteps, a promise that this man faithfully clung to despite his son's arrogant attitude and trajectory into law school. Years later, God's revelation compelled Wayne to change career paths and enter the ministry just like his dad. Given the prodigal nature of his journey, Wayne now stood as a testimony to his father's assertion: "Faith has bad days, but faith sees the end."

I believe the same can be said for praise. At times the night seems to last forever and we wonder whether the sun will ever rise again, but our choice to praise brings divine guidance in the darkness and sound hope when we're lost on life's stormy seas. Committing to honouring God's reality beyond the thunderclaps helps us declare in thought, word, and deed that this time we will follow the Lord irrespective of the season.

THE FIRST LITTLE BLUE PILL

The climax of this continuing hostility between Rachel and Leah came during the wheat harvest when Leah's oldest son Reuben went out to the fields and found some mandrake plants that he brought home for his mother. Anyone would be forgiven for wondering, "So what?"

In those times, mandrake roots were thought to be a cure for infertility. They also contained an aphrodisiac. I wonder, did this lead to an awkward mother-son conversation?

"Hey, son, could you go out in the field and find me a few mandrakes?"

"Why, Mom?"

"Ahhhh… I'll tell you when you're older."

For the bickering sisters, mandrake roots were a powerful bargaining chip. Rachel had asked Leah for a few of the roots to prepare her oven, in a manner of speaking. This request was met with fury: *"Wasn't it enough that you took away my husband? Will you take my son's mandrakes too?"* (Genesis 30:15) The compensation, Rachel angrily retorted, was that Jacob would sleep with her that night.

Wow! How romantic.

So without his knowledge or consent, Jacob became the pawn, the mandrakes the fuel, and the kids collateral as sisterly sparks lit up the night sky. What more could happen?

As the sisters' deal was ratified, Jacob came home from a hard day's work. Instead of being gently wooed by Leah, she demanded his body strictly for its child-making abilities. Endearingly, Leah said, *"You must sleep with me… I have hired you with my son's mandrakes"* (Genesis 30:16).

Let's allow the steam to settle in as we draw a quick comparison.

The house behind our back fence belongs to a young family with a three-year-old boy whose demeanour is directly dependent on whether he gets what he demands from his parents. When he does, he's super happy. When a treat is denied or access to the trampoline barred, he has a tantrum of epic proportions. Soon after, he settles and the world returns to the way it should be—until the next eruption.

While each person's rate of development is different, I do wonder whether this reaction is somewhat indicative of how we treat our heavenly Father. Does our praise follow a similar emotional equation to the one demonstrated by my juvenile neighbour? Thank God that His grace and mercy aren't manipulated by our erratic outbursts or demands for selfish comforts. Our heavenly Father loves us far too much for such capitulation. He shows His unending love for us through godly discipline and transcendent wisdom in giving us all that we need according to His perfect plan and purpose.

The hard days of praise are very real, my friends. I'm right there with you. And yet our journey towards spiritual maturity challenges us to honour God for who He is without exception. He knows our hurts, fears, and questions and longs for us to embrace His perspective in seeing past these temporary hurdles for the joy of His sovereign character. Sometimes we lose a battle here and there, but the war is already secured in Jesus's defeat of death and the grave.

So after a battle wound, let's get up off the ground and stand again with praise to our champion for His all-surpassing power and eternal grace.

A Grace-Covered Past

From the past to the future, God's love and grace are limitless. He brings us back around the block as often as we need in life's journey. We constantly receive His undeserved favour.

And this is Leah's testimony also, as Genesis 30:17 shows God listening to Leah and granting her another pregnancy. In fact, she went on to birth three more children, two sons and a daughter, in the years to come while recycling the same futile pattern in naming her sons: Issachar means *"God has rewarded me for giving my servant to my husband"*

(Genesis 30:18) and Zebulun means *"God has presented me with a precious gift. This time my husband will treat me with honor, because I have borne him six sons"* (Genesis 30:19).

The final member of Leah's tribe was a daughter named Dinah, who was born with little documented fanfare.

Can you see the pattern of name associations? It feels like we're back to where we started. Leah focused on her self-centred actions and desired outcomes instead of choosing to celebrate God's continued blessing with unidirectional praise.

Regression is a trait common to humanity, including in our Christian walk. Why? Because our fleshly spirit is constantly at war with God's spirit in us, which is renewed daily to emulate Jesus (Colossians 3:10). Whichever one we feed more gains ascendancy in the battle.

Praise God for His mercy, which never lets us go or grows frustrated with our flipflopping antics.

Sometimes I look at myself in the light of God's call and feel disheartened. I wonder, "How did I regress to this point again?" Looking at the size of our dilemma compared to God's call for us can produce a downward spiral. Though don't allow shame to devalue your spiritual development. From a humble posture, praise God on your knees for His limitless forgiveness, enduring love, and abundant mercy. He is forever our ultimate source of hope in achieving what He has predestined us for in and through Jesus, who stands faithfully beside us to intercede to our Father whatever the circumstance.

Luke 22:31–32 confirms this. During the last supper, Jesus says to his disciple and friend,

> Simon, Simon, Satan has asked to sift each of you like wheat. But I have pleaded in prayer for you, Simon, that your faith should not fail. So when you have repented and turned to me again, strengthen your brothers. (NLT)

Jesus let Simon know that a spiritual tsunami was on the horizon. The result was that he would crash and burn before being reconciled to

Jesus again and use this as a testimony for the disciples. In one statement, this was both a dagger to the heart and a promise.

Read on in the text to watch this beautiful revelation come to pass. It's so relatable for us today. Jesus makes it clear that Satan is intent on our demise. He wants to grind us into the dirt. Take a breath, though, and let your spirit soar; Jesus says that He holds us securely in His prayerful embrace. What an amazing truth!

Jesus knew that Simon would stumble, but His grace would never reject Simon. This would serve as a permanent example for the generations to come.

Today Jesus wants to remind us of the same. Though we stumble in our faith, He who has seen the end is cheering for us. He prays His restorative strength into us and gives us the Holy Spirit as our divine Helper. Today and forever, Jesus stands with us and says, "I know your mistakes, but My love for you is wider, deeper, and higher than anything you have ever done or could ever do." His arms of love are open wide.

So claim your forgiveness, stand to your feet, accept Jesus's healing restoration, feel the Holy Spirit's wind at your back, and use your restorative testimony of grace to help lift another's eyes and heart above their own sense of failure. Extend praise forever to our Saviour and King, who is perpetually available for everyone who calls on the name of the Lord.

LOVE TRANSFORMING OUR BROKENNESS

Author, entrepreneur, and motivational speaker Emanuel "Jim" Rohn has said, "We all must suffer one of two pains: the pain of discipline or the pain of regret. What we suggest to everybody is to consider the disciplines because disciplines weigh ounces; regrets weigh tons."[25] Following God certainly requires a degree of discipline that comes with many great benefits, such as what we experience through praise, while the comparative pain of rejecting his offer will produce an eternity of regret.

I saw this dilemma play out before my eyes while working as a radiation therapist in Brisbane, Australia for almost a decade. It was an honour to treat cancer patients with high-voltage X-rays for the purpose

---

[25] Jim Rohn, "Being Successful Is a Personal Choice," *Jim Rohn*. Date of access: July 29, 2025 (https://www.jimrohn.com/success-is-a-personal-choice).

of cure or palliation to improve their quality of life, according to the doctor's determination.

While treating one patient, a fifty-year-old man, the electronics on our linear accelerator failed, as sometimes happened. The temporary pause allowed us to chat while the electronics team rectified the issue.

During our conversation, this gentleman shared openly that his doctor was very confident of a bright outcome for him. He felt further encouragement from having reconciled his relationship with his family and being promoted at work. In short, he had a new lease on life.

In fact, everything seemed so great for this intrepid patient that I was caught completely off-guard when his demeanour abruptly changed and tears welled up in his eyes. As we sat together in silence, it felt like a profoundly sacred moment.

After a few deep breaths, this man asked a haunting question that continues to motivate my Christian mission to this day. In the confines of our intimate environment, he asked, "So tell me: if everything is going amazingly well, why am I still so broken?"

I honestly can't remember my response to this man laying bare his heart. I continue to pray that he will one day have a personal relationship with Jesus, as he had exhausted all other possibilities yet found no answer to his emptiness.

This question, though, was foundational in catalyzing my movement from radiation therapy into counselling, pastoring, and chaplaincy. While I learned greatly from this career, I sensed a calling to help people holistically, not just to help meet their physical needs. I firmly believe that these divine cracks in our sometimes-glossy personas create the perfect entry point to deepen our relationship with the Author of our stories and Healer of our souls.

This divine relationship can start through a vulnerable God-orchestrated conversation that allows us to see each other and speak the Holy Spirit's words of hope and life into people with even the toughest exteriors. God created each of us with an innate need to be connected, loved, and known by others in serving as His representatives. We have all been created with a God-sized hole in our hearts. Unless we intentionally invite Him to fill this void and do what only He can, no amount of self-help, success, or striving will ever quench this need.

THE ROLE OF THE BODY

As Christ-followers, we have been empowered with an amazing opportunity. James 5:16 says, *"So confess your sins to one another and pray for one another so that you may be healed"* (NET). God is the only one who can save us, through Jesus, yet in His wisdom He enables us to stand in proxy for Him in offering the divine ministry of healing and reconciliation.

The power to request and offer God's forgiveness through confession requires both humility and courage. There can be a dangerous allure in harbouring bitterness towards others and seeking to maintain the moral high ground when we feel unjustly wronged. Self-justification and bitterness can truly hold us hostage if we fail to forgive and release justice into God's hands.

Our enemy concocts this sly plan to isolate us through hurt and offence, yet nothing destroys the power of shame or arrogance like intentionally choosing to move towards God and community.

Jesus's earthly half-brother, James, would have had a front row seat in watching the Son of God navigate three decades of everyday life before the beginning of his three-year ministry. I wonder what James observed when Jesus maybe incorrectly assembled a shelf in the carpentry shop? How did Jesus respond after receiving parental discipline when he went missing for three days during the Passover feast? I suspect that James's accumulated wisdom led him to write, *"Understand this, my dear brothers and sisters: You must all be quick to listen, slow to speak, and slow to get angry"* (James 1:19, NLT) Why? Because our human reaction can be to argue, make excuses, justify our actions, play the victim, or attack another's character and credibility. Our raw emotions may seethe just beneath the surface, and they're often indicative of a far deeper issue festering in our lives.

By contrast, those with a humble posture listen without arguing or needing to defend themselves. They carefully consider their words, sift wisdom from the pain, and gently seek to offer a measured response in alignment with God's heart for everyone's benefit.

Through daily surrender to God's sovereignty, our seemingly hopeless circumstances will transform all things into the shape of His perfect plans. Our loving heavenly Father is forever in control and always at work to redeem all things through His infinite ability to heal and restore.

Let's commit to doing whatever is possible to graciously forgive and wisely move forward while trusting God's limitless ability to transform the issues outside our control.

Designed for Connection

Make no mistake: the completion of God's plans in our lives doesn't happen in isolation; it always happens in community. He has designed us for relationship, connection, cooperation, and intimacy with Himself and others. We function best in a synergistic social setting to accomplish far more than we could individually. Partnering with other faithful friends on God's corporate mission leads to incredible outcomes that exceed anything we could ask, think, or imagine for the praise of His glory, as promised in Ephesians 3:20.

Yes, it's inevitable that we'll get hurt, and hurt others, in these community relationships, but God predominately designed us to find healing and spur growth. God's wisdom, through King Solomon, reminds us, *"Wounds from a sincere friend are better than many kisses from an enemy"* (Proverbs 27:6, NLT). Wise rebuke spoken in love is far better than endless flattery, which leads to destruction. We would do well to remember that God disciplines those He loves (Hebrews 12:6). He sometimes uses our own faith family to help us identify and correct important blind spots. These can be painful yet necessary lessons.

Through a counselling lens, this can be articulated as either clean or dirty pain. Dirty pain is like having a large splinter in your foot that prevents you from most forms of activity. It causes pain when triggered, but you fear the pain associated with its removal more than you look forward to renewing your previous lifestyle.

The alternative is clean pain, which is endured as the foreign body is removed. Yet after the extraction, you are unhindered in continuing the purpose to which you were called.

The common element is pain, though our engagement with it will have vastly different outcomes based on our choice.

Sometimes a loving and caring friend is called to humbly illuminate and remove blockages that prevent us from reaching our godly potential. Can it hurt? Yes, but usually it's temporary. We help each other walk the path, process issues, and overcome blind spots in our lives. Truth be told, we're often only one step away from making stupid mistakes on any given day without the benefit of a brother or sister's godly insight in boldly speaking the Holy Spirit's message to us. Grace flows in and through our lives as we humbly submit to one another in authentic relationships.

I suspect this was one of the primary flaws in Leah's spiritual paralysis. Who did she have in her corner asking the tough questions, offering wise counsel, and helping her walk God's intended path towards freedom? Spiritual accountability is an important part of the equation for living transparently in community with other Christ-followers.

Do you have someone who will ask you the tough questions in love because they care deeply about your growth trajectory and divine purpose? The wisdom of Ecclesiastes reads, *"A person standing alone can be attacked and defeated, but two can stand back-to-back and conquer. Three are even better, for a triple-braided cord is not easily broken"* (Ecclesiastes 4:12, NLT).

In his book *Walking with Lions*, pastor Jonathan Wiggins asks a profound question: who do you run with and what is their influence on you?[26] The old proverb that "you are what you eat" can be expanded to consider how friendships progressively mould us as we spend time with other influences. Proverbs 13:20 puts it this way: *"Keep company with the wise and you will become wise. If you make friends with stupid people, you will be ruined"* (GNT). And according to 1 Corinthians 15:33, *"Do not be misled: 'Bad company corrupts good character'"* (1 Corinthians 15:33).

The fact is that the friends you keep regular company with will strongly influence your future! This also applies to friends who help you praise the Lord both individually and in community.

---

[26] Jonathan Wiggins, *Walking with Lions* (Birmingham, AL: Association of Related Churches, 2021), 38.

Pay specific attention to the people you give the right to speak into your life and objectively assess the benefit of these relationships. This might mean making some hard decisions to release detrimental influences and having the courage to initiate new, life-giving relationships with those who are walking in a direction that matches the Holy Spirit's leading in your own life. Our effectiveness in achieving God's purpose is dependent on us synergistically partnering with those whom He positions us alongside, even though these relationships are rarely problem-free.

David would certainly testify to this principle, having fled from King Saul and taken refuge in the cave of Adullam. If finding solace in a cold, dank cave wasn't bad enough, God then "blessed" him with a large collection of misfits for company. No one looking for an encouraging band of brothers would choose this motley crew. As 1 Samuel 22:2 says, *"All those who were in distress or in debt or discontented gathered around him [David], and he became their commander. About four hundred men were with him."*

Several hundred poor, grumpy and panicked dudes… what perfect company!

But God had divinely orchestrated these partnerships for individual and mutual benefit. During this process, David learned the benefit of having deep relationships and learning godly lessons in leadership and conflict resolution. Being obedient to God's direction above his own feelings positioned him perfectly to become Israel's succeeding king.

Several chapters later, and many years after their initial rendezvous, David celebrates this same group of guys as his mighty men because of their selfless and heroic exploits. You can read all about King David's hall of fame picks in 2 Samuel 23:8–39.

It's so encouraging to reflect on how God takes our brokenness and progressively turns it into something infinitely more productive—that is, if we choose to follow His direction with praise. I would contend that these men weren't just all-stars when it came to military exploits, though. They also helped lift David's eyes to God in praise on occasions when he was in dire straits.

Let's passionately follow David's example and invest ourselves in God's divine relationships, which ultimately nourish, encourage, and sustain our godly purpose through all of life's seasons.

With God's purpose in you, Jesus leading you, the Holy Spirit empowering you towards praise, and godly friends surrounding you, it will make for an incredible journey. We each have a purpose far bigger than ourselves, one that God intended to use for His glory, and we get to do it together.

In seasons when praise is hard to honour, these continuously cultivated friendships help us share the load and focus our eyes on hope. And as with Moses, these godly mates can lift our hands and hearts to see God's face.

Relationships are God's incredible idea for us. Given such a gift, let's make the choice to praise God for and invest passionately in community.

Reflection Time

- Godly tenacity is inherent in the statement that faith and praise have bad days, but faith and praise see the end. Given our short memories, we need to remind ourselves often of God's past faithfulness. List five historical things to praise Him for today.

- While writing, consider any habitual patterns you've fallen prey to that cause praise to dry up in your life. Try documenting a strategy for the next time a similar event or attack occurs. Maybe it includes a friend you can call on to help fight discouragement or apathy.

- Using Luke 22:31–32 from The Passion translation, speak this verse aloud, inserting your own name in the blanks, and listen closely to hear Jesus prayer over you: "_____, my dear friend, listen to what I'm about to tell you. Satan has obtained permission to come and sift you all like wheat and test your faith. But I have prayed for you, _____, that you would stay faithful to me no matter what comes. Remember this: after you have turned back to me and have been restored, make it your life mission to strengthen the faith of your brothers" (TBT).

- Who is in your corner to do this Christian journey alongside you? You need them, and they need you, to praise together and lean on one another. Make time this week to call, text, or connect with them to thank them for their friendship. Commit yourself to helping with God's purpose in and through them too.

7

Judah's Unfolding Story

*For no matter how many promises God has made, they are
"Yes" in Christ. And so through him the "Amen" is spoken
by us to the glory of God.* (2 Corinthians 1:20)

Ingrained in my DNA is a passion for long-distance activities. While I don't aspire to run an ultramarathon or compete in the Hawaiian Ironman, I was a competitive swimmer (400/800-metre freestyle specialist), which morphed into some smaller triathlons, ten-kilometre events, and half-marathons. While Kristy thinks I'm a little crazy, and probably with good reason, I savour the opportunity to systematically focus on different aspects of my technique over a race's duration.

Similarly, I find enjoyment in watching home improvement shows. They're very inspiring, with each episode documenting the long journey of an individual, couple, or family being mentored by a professional to plan and build their dream home. In one such show, *Grand Designs*, this process can last up to seven years, with the host checking in with them periodically to celebrate their successes and help navigate the challenges inherent in the campaign. Most episodes culminate with the exuberant homeowners standing in front of their newly constructed masterpieces, with the former difficulties now just a distant memory.

This type of sustained reporting is called a *longitudinal study*, where projects are observed repeatedly over an extended period. Longitudinal studies are often used for medical research, psychological studies, or sociological disciplines to monitor and assess people's progress over time.

Praise has numerous similarities. The Holy Spirit constantly invites us to this discipline while supplying wise counsel and divine strength at every juncture.

Let's turn our focus to Leah's fourth son, Judah, to better understand how his birthname and experience intersect across a longitudinal study of praise.

Passing the Baton Forward

Judah's name is regularly mentioned in the later chapters of Genesis, given his frequent interactions with his biological siblings and half-brothers, the most well-known being Joseph, the oldest of Rachel's two birthed sons (Genesis 30:22–24).

Early in his life, Judah made regular and relatable mistakes while struggling to own and embody his God-given name. Please don't think that God or Leah made an error in bestowing this name on him, though. Just like you and me, our loving Father calls us by our own heavenly name that doesn't initially fit our messy earthly persona. We need time, grace, tenacity, and His divine help to grow into it.

Genesis 37 records the story of Joseph from his father Jacob's perspective. Joseph is the guy who was given a stunningly ornate coat by his dad—and this story is interspersed with several insightful appearances by Judah.

According to the biblical text, seventeen-year-old Joseph made several passionate utterances that strained relationships within his family and landed him in all sorts of trouble. Given modern research that says the male brain isn't fully developed until the age of twenty-five, perhaps this shouldn't come as a big surprise.

Seemingly oblivious to his brothers' escalating jealousy, Joseph prophetically blurted out two God-given dreams which provoked Judah to rally his brothers and catalyze Joseph's sale into slavery for a few bucks. This seemed more lucrative than the brothers' original plan, which had been to kill him. As the natural leader of the group, Judah seemed to call the shots and serve as the brothers' spokesman.

The Genesis account briefly focuses on Judah's decisions, showing him leave his family to marry Shua, a Canaanite woman. The Canaanites were the Israelites' religious enemies.

Judah and Shua had three sons together—Er, Onan, and Shelah. As this trio matured into adulthood, Judah found a wife for his oldest son, a woman named Tamar. As it turned out, Er was extremely evil in God's sight and was divinely obliterated.

The cultural imperative in those days was that the next son by birth order—in this case, Onan—was obligated to marry his widowed sister-in-law and continue the family lineage. The story goes that Onan wasn't too keen on propagating his brother's bloodline and deliberately spilled his semen on the ground when sleeping with Tamar. This was also very wicked in God's sight, so he ended Onan's life too.

Judah was fast running out of sons as suitable husbands for Tamar. He told her to live as a widow at her parents' house until Shelah was ready for marriage. The two-time widow honoured Judah's request for a long time, as the Bible describes it.

But with Judah not in a hurry to make any marriage arrangement, Tamar eventually hatched a devious plan. Hearing that Judah was busy shearing his sheep one day, she exchanged her widow's clothes and covered her face like a temple prostitute, then blatantly positioned herself along Judah's regular route home. Judah took the bait and solicited her, unknowingly offering his daughter-in-law payment for sex.

Tamar cunningly asked Judah for his staff, signet ring, and cord as an interim payment for his temporary pleasure. These emblems were the historical equivalent of holding one's driver's license, credit card, and social insurance number. She shrewdly held these articles as leverage for the next phase of her plan.

When the headlines broke that Tamar was pregnant, Judah demanded that she be publicly exposed and burned at the stake. But the joke was on him when Tamar revealed that Judah himself was the father of her imminent child. Aghast at this change of circumstance, Judah was forced to confess that Tamar was more honourable than he since he hadn't really intended on giving Shelah to her in marriage as he'd originally promised. What an R-rated twist!

A Return to Egypt

Shortly thereafter, a ravenous famine swept the globe, forcing everyone to flee to Egypt for food, as this was the only country in existence with a prolific nutritional supply. The caveat was that all food requests had to be approved by the kingdom's second-in-command—none other than Joseph. Yes, the very same guy Judah and company had sold into slavery years earlier.

Since Jacob's extended family was struggling for survival, the brothers hurriedly arranged a rescue mission to secure supplies from Egypt. As Judah and the others stood humbly before the nation's governor, they didn't recognize him as their half-brother Joseph since he had seamlessly assimilated into Egyptian culture over the past two decades.

But he knew exactly who they were.

Maybe Joseph harboured a small chip on his shoulder as he recognized his brothers and chose to interrogate them more harshly than the other fugitives. He then declared them to be spies and a probable threat to national security.

After holding them in prison for three days, Joseph gave the group an ultimatum: one of the brothers, Simeon, would remain imprisoned while the rest raced back home to get their youngest brother, Benjamin, to secure Simeon's release. Benjamin, Jacob's youngest and Rachel's only remaining biological son, was incredibly significant to Jacob.

The brothers returned home and implored Jacob that they needed to return to Egypt with Benjamin as soon as possible if they wanted to secure food. The grieving Jacob, devoid of alternatives, lamented that his life would be over if harm were to befall his beloved son.

Genesis 43:8–9 reveals that Judah vouched for Benjamin's safety and used his own life as a guarantee. Wow! What a remarkable transformation Judah underwent in his progressive journey to embody his divine name.

A Change Is in the Wind

I feel like I can relate to Judah. Though I never sold my brother into slavery, I remember many thousand-kilometre family road trips to Sydney at Christmas to celebrate the season with family and friends. The drive could be monotonous and long and we often napped to pass the time.

On one particular trip, when I was about twelve, I distinctly remember trying to stay awake so I could be available for Dad should he need anything while Mum and my siblings slept. It was a heavy weight of self-imposed responsibility, but I was willing to shoulder it out of love and for the safety and security of our family.

Praise can be projected through these types of scenarios in honouring God while also honing our character towards selflessness and surrender.

Judah assured his father that if anything were to go wrong during the rescue mission, he alone would forever bear the blame. How had this journey towards praise evolved in Judah's heart? No doubt a multitude of emotions were coursing through his body, yet he rose above these dire circumstances and resolved to act as Benjamin's bodyguard. He was laying everything down for the sake of another.

Upon the brothers' return to Egypt, they gained an audience with the governor. When Joseph saw Benjamin, he freed Simeon from prison and all seemed peachy—that is, until the brothers secured their needed food and prepared to head back home.

Just before their departure, another plot twist occurred. Joseph cunningly ordered that his own silver goblet be hidden in Benjamin's food sack.

The brothers had barely left the city limits when Joseph raised the alarm with his council that these Israelite traitors had repaid his generosity with greed and theft. The brothers were pursued, arrested, and systematically searched for the prized article.

Given their pure motives and clear conscience, the brothers wholeheartedly agreed to the search, insisting that they wouldn't have stolen the chalice. And if they did, the guilty party should be executed immediately, with the remaining men becoming the governor's slaves for life.

So imagine their sheer panic when the coveted emblem was discovered in Benjamin's possession! These guys were most certainly up the creek without anything resembling a paddle.

In an act of selfless surrender, Judah tangibly personified praise as he entered the palace to intercede for his half-brother Benjamin. Genesis 44:33 records Judah speaking to his still-disguised brother Joseph, saying, *"Now then, please let your servant remain here as my lord's slave in place of the boy, and let the boy return with his brothers."*

How incredible! Judah asked for his own life to be given as a ransom for his brother. Here he stood as a divinely transformed servant of God, radically different from his previous self when he had craved financial gain above grace and lust above integrity.

As with Judah, praise urges us along the path of spiritual maturity. It sharpens our godly eyesight and transforms our hearts to honour God's voice above our own. As we commit our time, talents, and treasures in praise of the One completely deserving of them all, our lives reciprocally grow deeper and richer. The Holy Spirit grants us the ability to perceive His motives and our lives become a joyful surrender in the humble acknowledgement of all that Jesus has given us.

Could Judah's selfless and humble request to Joseph be a foreshadowing of Jesus's heart and divine plan, something that wouldn't occur until many generations later?

Praise God that our toxic guilt has been redeemed in exchange for Jesus's perfect innocence, our freedom generously purchased through His divine sacrifice.

A Heart Bursting with Praise

How can we respond to such a priceless gift? How do we honour our profound indebtedness? Romans 5:8 captures the exact outpouring of gratitude: *"But God demonstrates his own love for us in this: While we were still sinners, Christ died for us."*

The best and only response we can offer God is the humble gift of lifting our hands in praise, surrendering to the King of Kings and Lord of Lords now and forever for His unfathomable grace that can never be repaid.

As mentioned earlier, the term *Hallelujah* brags about the greatness of God. Though it's a meagre offering in the absence of anything befitting our Saviour and Lord, it's all we have to offer. This recalls the deepest heart cry of the psalmist: *"Why am I discouraged? Why is my heart so sad? I will put my hope in God! I will praise him again—my Savior and my God!"* (Psalm 42:5–6, 43:5, NLT)

When we give ourselves completely to God, He honours our offering with a gift of freedom we can barely comprehend. Similarly, as Judah surrendered his body to death or indefinite captivity, God sovereignly stepped in and changed his ominous trajectory for His glory, as a praise testimony that would mark Judah across his lifetime.

Until now, Joseph had been unrecognizable as their half-brother, the biological son of Rachel, nephew of Leah, and scapegoat of his brothers' anger, resentment, and jealousy. Yet as he stood before Judah as second-in-command of Egypt, preparing to pronounce judgment, he went radically off-script. He cleared the room of servants and with loud weeping got ready to reveal his true identity.

Let's take a pause right here. What do you suspect Judah was thinking at this juncture? As the brothers awaited the governor's judgment, their attention was stolen by a completely unexpected statement:

> Come close to me… I am your brother Joseph, the one you sold into Egypt! And now, do not be distressed and do not be angry with yourselves for selling me here, because it was to save lives that God sent me ahead of you. (Genesis 45:4–5)

Ahhhh… say what? At what point do you suspect these brothers needed to pick their jaws up off the floor? To help them process the magnitude of this mind-blowing reversal, Joseph twice repeated the truth—that God had sent him to Egypt ahead of them to preserve a remnant of Israel according to His divine plan.

Talk about a cosmic plot twist! This man, highly enthroned in Egypt, had himself spent several years captive in Pharaoh's prison while he underwent a radical personal transformation similar to Judah's. Praise the God of perpetual goodness who operates far above our thoughts, hopes, and dreams.

Let's fast-forward the story. Joseph received permission from Pharaoh to expedite the physical relocation and reunification of his whole family to Egypt by providing carts for the journey and assigning a nearby territory for them to live in abundance and prosperity.

Pay special attention to this incredible detail in the story: while enroute to Egypt, Jacob sent Judah ahead to get directions from Joseph to their new home in Goshen (Genesis 46:28). Isn't it awesome that praise led this advance party to connect with the reunifying power of transformation in confirming the family's future home? What a phenomenal praise testimony!

We can never fathom exactly what God's plans might be, but one thing we know for sure: His outcome is forever good, even though it may look and feel very different than what we imagined. Praise must therefore be our only possible offering for Him. It celebrates God's faithful character, plans, and love from eternity past to eternity future, irrespective of anything we could ever add from our own merit. Praise the Lord for His unending love and immeasurable grace!

So where do you find yourself right now? Are you in a season of intense gratitude or maybe feeling overwhelmed by darkness? Maybe you have ongoing challenges physically, emotionally, mentally, relationally, or spiritually. If so, here is a special message from the sovereign God of the universe just for you.

The One you have just read about, the One whom we have the unmerited privilege of calling Father and Saviour, spoke this truth-filled reminder through the prophet Isaiah of His surprises in the depths of our despair: *"And I will give you treasures hidden in the darkness—secret riches. I will do this so you may know that I am the Lord, the God of Israel, the one who calls you by name"* (Isaiah 45:3, NLT). Our Almighty God, who does not lie (Hebrews 6:17–19), says, He has hidden His gift of goodness even in our darkness. Why? So that we will know the steadfast hope that He alone is God and wants us to experience His love in every season of our lives, even in the pit of despair.

Take a moment to praise Him for His faithful goodness, whether you're experiencing this today or His promises remain hidden for now. Listen closely as He calls you by name—not just your earthly name, but according to the name He has reserved for you, the version of yourself into which He is consistently transforming you. Just like with Judah, He is calling you back to Himself, deeper into the perfect plan He customized for you.

Similar to how Joseph called for his brothers to come close to him, so your loving heavenly Father invites you to come close, for He has more for you than you could ever imagine, irrespective of the reality you see today. Praise God for His heart, which forgives our past, empowers our present, and transcends our future according to His eternal goodness.

God's Refining Trials

Romans 5:3–5 is one of those challenging yet inspirational passages of the Scripture that calls us to decisive action in remembering God's goodness. Our intentional effort is also required to apprehend this godly posture, given the challenging seasons we pass through.

The apostle Paul boldly declared, amidst his own difficulties,

> Not only this, but we also rejoice in sufferings, knowing that suffering produces endurance, and endurance, character, and character, hope. And hope does not disappoint, because the love of God has been poured out in our hearts through the Holy Spirit who was given to us. (Romans 5:3–5, NET)

Do you see the progression here? Suffering, when seasoned with rejoicing and praise, becomes a vehicle of diligent tenacity that fosters the consistent development of godly character in us and transforms into God's unshakable hope. What an inspiring equation to hold onto when the journey becomes difficult!

God uses broken people and messy situations to showcase the extraordinary aspects of His faithful character to the world. And while our praise often presents as deficient, the Holy Spirit miraculously transforms our praise offerings into sweet-smelling sacrifices that give honour to the One who deserves the highest glory.

Maybe your offerings of praise have become contingent on what you hope to receive through a divine exchange, but right now is the perfect time to begin to renew true unidirectional praise.

My personal life became very broken in June 2021, with the COVID-19 pandemic upending everything. One morning, while pouring my heart out to God, a rush of heavenly revelation lodged in my spirit. I heard this phrase: "My bride is still being prepared in the dark."

An image sprang to my mind—a bride getting ready for her wedding day in the middle of a power outage. Such an event would be disastrous for any bride, maybe even necessitating a postponement. Yet by overlaying my new spiritual revelation over my current predicament, I felt that the Holy Spirit was saying to me that Jesus doesn't abandon us in the darkness of our despair. Our divine wedding and bridal waltz continue, even amidst the evil that surrounds us. Jesus alone purifies our brokenness so we can stand before Him without stain or blemish. He alone escorts us into the radiance of God's holy presence with a song of pure praise (Ephesians 5:25–27).

God's church includes everyone past, present, and future; together, we form the bride of Christ and are daily being prepared for our eternal union with Jesus in heaven.

In the same way, trials will come, and they will resolve in due season, but praise to our Lord and Saviour will remain unyielding in all seasons given the unchanging nature of our God, who commands transcendent goodness in every circumstance for the honour of His name.

THE OBJECT OF OUR PRAISE

Our God-centred praise is anchored by the sure knowledge that we have been created for the amplification of His love to all humanity. Think about some of the self-centric questions we ask in life. What do I want to be when I grow up? Who do I want to marry? Where do I want to live? What should I do when I retire?

Are such questions wrong? Of course not. But constantly focusing on ourselves can add a layer of separation between our true selves and the reason we are here. It's not primarily about us. God is calling us out of our self-centredness into His purpose-filled destiny to praise Him and help others. Without this mandate fuelling our godly resolve, our lives will lack sustainable purpose.

Rick Warren's *The Purpose Driven Life* speaks to this:

> It's not about you. The purpose of your life is far greater than your own personal fulfillment, your peace of mind, or even your own happiness. It's far greater than your family, your career, or even your wildest dreams and ambitions. If you want to know why you were placed here on this planet, you must begin with God. You were born by his purpose and for his purpose.[27]

Characters throughout the Bible were also tempted to lose themselves in self-consumed thoughts versus offering a constant sacrifice of praise. In Daniel 4:30, King Nebuchadnezzar reigned over the most powerful city in the ancient world. Listen to his boast: *"Look at this great city of Babylon! By my own mighty power, I have built this beautiful city as my royal residence to display my majestic splendor"* (NLT)

Okay, so maybe our own boasts aren't quite as grandiose as this. But sometimes my sense of entitlement selfishly elevates my achievements, needs, and desires above everyone else's, including God's.

If this self-centric posture remains unchallenged and our God-directed praise evaporates from our lives, we will quickly come to the end of ourselves. So either we learn this foundational principle by making a humble decision or God can step in and teach us by His power.

Nebuchadnezzar was singing a very different tune after God brought him down to size. After the recalibration of his God-given power and position, he praised and honoured the almighty King and Lord of heaven and earth, saying, *"His dominion is an eternal dominion; his kingdom*

---

[27] Rick Warren, *The Purpose Driven Life* (Grand Rapids, MI: Zondervan, 2002), 17.

endures from generation to generation… No one can hold back his hand" (Daniel 4:34–35, NLT).

We are called to build God's kingdom, not our own. Likewise, our praise is forever due His name, not ours.

With this theme in mind, the metanarrative of the Bible is that characters like Leah, Judah, and Nebuchadnezzar are not the heroes. They're like windows through which we look to see the Saviour. They simply help point us toward the true object of our praise.

There is only One who reigns as the hero. Jesus, heaven's champion, came to earth to show us the Father's love and died a sinner's death in our place. He came as Saviour because we couldn't save ourselves. Praise God for the all-surpassing life, love, and freedom He makes available for anyone who humbles themselves to accept His gracious gift.

Each of these biblical lives and testimonies points back to Him. And together with them we give our offering of praise to the One who was, is, and is to come. Hallelujah!

This I Know to Be True

When we choose to fix our eyes on Jesus with consistent intentionality, giving Him praise for who He is irrespective of our circumstances, we begin to see that His heart of love and wisdom is forever guiding us for His glory. The Holy Spirit's insight helps us to realize that every season has a purpose, nothing is wasted, and there is a divine process at work in order to see this purpose accomplished. The importance of this divine process acknowledges a pathway through pain and beckons us to cooperate with our temporal discomfort enroute to a God-orchestrated finale. The alternative is to live as victims in the valley of tears.

In *Hope in the Dark*, pastor Craig Groeschel concludes that our call to praise is a matter of perspective. This concept is beautifully depicted in a poem written by one of his fifteen-year-old congregants, Kyle McCarty:

> God doesn't love me
> You can't force me to believe
> God is good

This is the One Truth in life
This world is a product of chance
How can I believe that
God will use my life
I know with certainty that
God has left me
Never again will I say that
Christ is risen from the dead
I know now more than ever in my life that
Man can save himself
We must realise that it is ignorant to think
God answers prayers
Christians declare that
Without God this world would fall into darkness
This world can and will meet my needs
It is a lie to say that
God has always been there for me
I now realise that
No matter what I do
The Truth is
He doesn't love me
How can I presume that
God is good [28]

Feeling encouraged? No? Neither was I when I first read it!

But I'm asking you to reread this poem. This time, read it in reverse, starting with the last line. I'll wait here while you do.

What a huge difference that makes! And so it is with life. When all the injustices and hurts of this world assault our faith, it can be hard to praise God for who He is. Remember this statement by Philip Yancey: "faith [and praise] means trusting in advance what will only make sense in reverse."[29]

---

[28] Craig Groeschel, *Hope in the Dark* (Grand Rapids, MI: Zondervan, 2018), 149–150.

[29] Philip Yancey, "The Long View," *Philip Yancey.* June 2023 (https://philipyancey.com/the-long-view).

In walking by faith instead of being driven by our emotions, we can choose to embody a radically different understanding of God's nature and His purpose in the waiting. Every time this happens, take note and memorialize it. Hold this as sacred gift in your heart and allow these reflections to fuel your praise for today and tomorrow, for the next trial and the next challenging season, knowing that God is forever in charge and guiding you towards His best future for you.

POP QUIZ

Do you remember Judah's great-grandfather? Yes, it was Abraham. For those who got it correct, cash in your answer at your local convenience store for a free chocolate bar—but please pay the retail price before consuming it.

Recall that Abraham's wife Sarah was barren, yet God had promised Abraham that a nation would come from him. This was an unlikely scenario by human abilities, yet as Paul wrote in Romans 4:18, *"Against all hope, Abraham in hope believed and so became the father of many nations, just as it had been said to him, 'So shall your offspring be.'"*

Abraham chose to praise and believe God's version of the future over the reality he lived in. Praise informed his sure belief in God's divine purpose.

Leah chose to praise God for who He was despite the challenges that surrounded her.

Likewise, Judah progressively evolved into his name of praise while walking the path God had ordained for him.

And the same can be true of us as we begin to employ praise as our primary response to our Creator and Sustainer. With diligent rehearsing of this spiritual discipline, a more intimate and mature relationship will develop between us and our loving heavenly Father, one that exudes trust, love, and service that epitomize our divine transformation, and it's marked by praise.

So what happened to Leah and Judah, you may be asking? Well, join me in the penultimate chapter to find out, for this miraculous story is far from finished.

REFLECTION TIME

- There were many times when Judah didn't seem to fit with his God-given name. This became a daily choice. God used Judah despite all his mess, and He plans to do the same with us. Will you allow God to use your broken and possibly unfinished story for His praise?

- Our brokenness has a specific and godly purpose. In seeing the whole biblical narrative, we can see how God's faithfulness intersects with our faithlessness. What is one Bible verse or God-given truth you can use in your own praise offering today?

- Take time this week to listen to Brandon Lake's song "Gratitude." After listening, write down a few lines of your own praise for all that God has done, is doing, and promises to do.

- God faithfully purposes to use our story for His glory. Choose one person or situation this week and commit to praising God each time these come to mind, knowing that He is El Shaddai, the all-sufficient One (Genesis 17:1–2).

A Divine Genealogy

One generation will praise Your works to another, and will declare Your mighty acts. (Psalm 145:4, NASB)

Honour God's work from the past, praise Him passionately today, and invest ahead into His kingdom through the next generation. This great advice always requires an intentional choice on our part to keep moving the ball up the field. Praise is forever our benchmark along this divine odyssey as we reflect on God's covenantal promises that have no expiration date. They are always perfectly in process.

Let me offer a quick review, starting with the life of Abraham. At age seventy-five, the Almighty told him that he and his barren wife Sarah would become a great nation (Genesis 12:1–3). God repeated this promise several times (Genesis 13:14–17, 15:4–6), yet its reality was yet to materialize when he was ninety-nine years old.

It's important to remember that the supreme designer of all creation, the master engineer of biology, is never limited by time or science. Abraham's praise offering forthrightly elevated his testimony of God's supreme power.

When Abraham reached the age of one hundred, God's faithful promise was fulfilled. It was twenty-five years in the making. The couple now had a son, Isaac, who became the first descendant of God's great nation.

Isaac then married Rebecca and had two sons, Esau and Jacob, the later of whom married our protagonist, Leah.

During Leah's life, she bore a total of six sons and one daughter to Jacob. But even towards the closing credits of her story, she knew that her husband didn't really love her, at least not in comparison to her sister Rachel.

However, Leah progressively embraced her godly purpose, taking a combination of forward and backward steps. She accepted what God had done for her instead of relying on her own feelings and attachment to her husband.

I am continually inspired by the people God chose to act as His divine messengers of transformation. They serve as friends and mentors for us today. I'm thinking about Moses begging God to choose someone else to lead. Yet he did so using God's strength. Then there's Gideon, the scaredy cat who led Israel's army to conquer the Midianites. And what about Jesus's motley crew of disciples, the sort of people you wouldn't bet on to begin a global revolution in creating our modern-day church?

Throughout all these highs and lows, these desert experiences and faith challenges, let's choose to follow Mary's example. In Luke 2:19, we read that she *"treasured all these things, giving careful thought to them and pondering them in her heart"* (AMP).

So when the sky is bleak and God's promises appear miniscule on the horizon, we can stand firm on the documented history of God's faithfulness and allow this reality to fuel our endless praise.

Now it's our turn. The countless generations who've lived before us have placed the baton in our hands, inspiring God's praise in our hearts. We are called to follow the God of history and look forward to the heavenly city whose architect and builder is faithfully constructing an eternal home for anyone who chooses to call Jesus their Saviour and Lord.

God's Honour Displayed

While life didn't always turn out the way she expected, hoped, or felt it should, Leah still chose to act on her praise commitment to God, even with a few stumbles here and there. But towards the later part of Genesis, Leah fades from the narrative with no significant fanfare. In fact, she barely warrants another mention.

Think of how many artists are never regarded as significant until after they're dead? While this analogy isn't exactly the same, there are some similarities.

The Bible doesn't specifically document the time of Leah's death, although there are indicators about her burial in Genesis 49:29–31. Jacob gave instructions to his children about his own imminent passing:

> Bury me with my fathers in the cave in the field of Ephron the Hittite, the cave in the field of Machpelah, near Mamre in Canaan, which Abraham bought along with the field as a burial place from Ephron the Hittite. There Abraham and his wife Sarah were buried, there Isaac and his wife Rebekah were buried, and there I buried Leah.

Did you see that! What a profound statement to remember.

Generations earlier, as documented in Genesis 23, Abraham purchased the field of Machpelah as a burial plot for himself and his wife. This same tomb became a mausoleum for the succeeding duo of Isaac and Rebekah. And now Leah was honoured there as well, buried alongside this great lineage of the Messianic dynasty.

People have wondered why Rachel wasn't buried there too. The Bible says in Genesis 35:16–20 that she died giving birth to Benjamin and was buried beside the road enroute to Bethlehem.

While Leah's marriage began with deception and continued with the painful knowledge that she wasn't Jacob's preferred wife, at the end of her life Jacob honoured her by laying her to rest with her fellow matriarchs and patriarchs of the faith. God had chosen her to play a pivotal role in Jesus's generational heritage, an honour that would last throughout eternity.

Through Leah's story, we are reminded that a person's redemption isn't contingent on having the perfect marriage partner, an abundance of children, a plethora of good deeds, or an outstanding spiritual resume. Instead one's redemption occurs through adopting a humble heart fully surrendered to God's will. That's how we honour His glory.

Leah's six sons account for half of the founding representatives of Israel's twelve tribes. Despite her sometimes schizophrenic emotions, which we all have from time to time, I believe she knew that God had blessed her beyond what she deserved. As such, she gave Him the profound praise and honour due His name.

At the birth of her sixth son, Zebulun, the Bible records her as saying, *"God has endowed me with a good endowment…"* (Genesis 30:20, ESV) This word, endowment, can be translated as a gift or dowry. The implication is that God gave Leah an incredible gift of six sons, which stands as a praise testimony that He alone is exceedingly faithful throughout the twists and turns of life. Can I hear a rousing amen?

Praise Be to the Roaring Lion

Similar to Leah, Judah's sordid story is far from a spotless example of praise. Few might have expected him to be integral in this divine bloodline. But God's grace-filled plans are so radically different than ours. When God spoke the Holy-Spirit-inspired name of praise for Judah, this majestic pronouncement reverberated throughout history and on into eternity.

As Jacob knew his time on earth was fast elapsing, he called his sons together for one last group huddle and addressed each one according to a prophetically inspired revelation. The news wasn't that edifying for Reuben, Simeon, and Levi… so by the time he came to Judah, I'm sure this guy was anxiously and wondering what he could expect.

With a voice of godly authority, Jacob opened his mouth and declared,

> Judah, your brothers will praise you; your hand will be on the neck of your enemies; your father's sons will bow down to you. You are a lion's cub, Judah; you return from the prey, my son. Like a lion he crouches and lies down, like a lioness—who dares to rouse him? The scepter will not depart from Judah, nor the ruler's staff from between his feet, until he to whom it belongs shall come and the obedience of the nations shall be his. (Genesis 49:8–10)

Wow! Judah likely needed some time to process that holy download while the other brothers received their own divine messages.

Just to clarify, I'm no Bible scholar, but there are a few phrases here that stand out to me. Notice how the translation of Judah's name, praise, is first used for his own edification. He was a flawed man, but God determined that he would be revered by his siblings and the nations alike. That's a big deal, especially after Judah and his brothers had been forced to fall on their faces in abject fear a few years earlier upon unknowingly meeting Joseph in Egypt.

Furthermore, Judah was called a lion's cub, which makes me think of the opening scene from Disney's *The Lion King*. Can you imagine Jacob proudly lifting Judah by his armpits and parading him before all the family? No, me either, but that is the visual!

The reference to a lion's cub gains contextual significance when you jump from Genesis to Revelation 5:5 in the final book of the Bible. During his God-inspired vision, the apostle John is accompanied by one of heaven's elders. The elder says to John, *"Do not weep! See, the Lion of the tribe of Judah, the Root of David, has triumphed."* While Judah is referred to as a lion's cub, Jesus Christ is now hailed as the OG Lion, the Saviour of all humanity. To Him is ascribed the praise of heaven, since He has defeated death and the grave. Jacob's pronouncement over Judah was a God-breathed prophecy, with the kingly sceptre of power and authority travelling through Judah's lineage all the way to Jesus, the King of Kings, who now sits unchallenged on heaven's throne above every kingdom and authority for all eternity. Jesus is both all-powerful and yet extremely gentle, both the Lion of Judah and the lamb who was slain for the sin of all humanity to reconcile us to His Father, our Creator God.

The English language runs out of adjectives in describing the person of Jesus: trustworthy, powerful, merciful, caring, wisdom, strength, and limitless in His all-encompassing authority to rescue anyone who requests saving by declaring Him as their Saviour and Lord.

Amid the praise of heaven, another amazing reality is that God chooses to build His divine legacy through His church, including people like you and me, from generations past to generations ahead. His timeless promises are both personal and universal, applicable to everyone who follows His command. He unites us in the sure hope that together we will share in eternal life through Jesus. But more on that in a moment...

The Lineage of Jesus

The continuous celebration of Jesus as the Lion of Judah would not be complete without acknowledging the supporting cast members who predated His incarnation. Allow me to give a brief overview.

After Leah, Jacob, and Judah had died, the subsequent generations of Israelites were enslaved in Egypt for several hundred years. God chose a man called Moses to lead Israel out of slavery and into His preferred future for them in the promised land of Cannan.

Moses had an assistant named Joshua who led the nation after Moses died. In following God's direction, Israel came to the heavily fortified city of Jericho. Joshua commissioned two spies to scout out the city, and these men took refuge in the house of a prostitute named Rahab, who lived there with her family. She granted safety to the spies, since they represented the nation that Rahab knew by faith would conquer Jericho because of God's power. She exchanged their temporal safety for the sure promise of God's future provision and protection.

Joshua 2:12–14 records the dialogue between Rahab and the two spies.

> "Now then, please swear to me by the Lord that you will show kindness to my family, because I have shown

A DIVINE GENEOLOGY

kindness to you. Give me a sure sign that you will spare the lives of my father and mother, my brothers and sisters, and all who belong to them—and that you will save us from death."

"Our lives for your lives!" the men assured her. "If you don't tell what we are doing, we will treat you kindly and faithfully when the Lord gives us the land."

After God divinely flattened Jericho, Rahab and her family found a secure home among God's people. Divinely saved for God's future purposes, she married a man called Salmon from amongst the Israelites. Some commentators believe he may have been one of the two spies who scoped out Jericho. This pair later had son named Boaz (Matthew 1:5).

Another wonderous and interrelated story weaves through the biblical tapestry and culminates with an awe-inspiring crescendo. Recorded in the book of Ruth, a man from Bethlehem called Elimelech moved his family, including wife Naomi and sons Mahlon and Kilion, from the region of Judah in Israel to Moab to escape a devastating famine. Sound familiar? After the move, Elimelech died, and the two sons married local girls, Orpah and Ruth respectively.

Sadly, both brothers also died, leaving all three women widowed, destitute, and vulnerable.

Naomi then heard that the Lord had come to the aid of Israel, providing them with food.

> With her two daughters-in-law she left the place where she had been living and set out on the road that would take them back to the land of Judah. (Ruth 1:7).

The family had left Judah, the province of praise, in search of a better life, but they now embarked on a journey back. Doesn't that sound just like our God! He's our ultimate Restorer, redeeming our lives from the pit of pain and despair and bringing us back into His loving embrace!

Before the journey, Naomi encouraged both of her daughters-in-law to stay in Moab and remarry local husbands while she made the homeward journey to Judah solo. Orpah chose this option, but Ruth refused, insisting, *"Where you go I will go, and where you stay I will stay. Your people will be my people and your God my God. Where you die I will die, and there I will be buried"* (Ruth 1:16–17). Now that's commitment!

So Naomi and Ruth made tracks towards Judah. Upon reaching Bethlehem, the townswomen questioned whether this returning stranger was really Naomi, since they hadn't seen her in more than a decade. Maybe she had gained a few pounds, changed her hair, or was sporting a new outfit!

Naomi's response startled them:

> "Don't call me Naomi," she told them. "Call me Mara, because the Almighty has made my life very bitter. I went away full, but the Lord has brought me back empty. Why call me Naomi? The Lord has afflicted me; the Almighty has brought misfortune upon me." (Ruth 1:20–21)

That's pretty black and white. Have you ever felt like this, like God had failed you? Are you there now? If so, take a breath, open your heart, and read on. This is the same God who promises to bring beauty out of ashes for everyone who believes.

A few small details in this story give us amazing insight into God's heart, plans, and provision. The text reads that Naomi and Ruth arrived in Bethlehem *"as the barley harvest was beginning"* (Ruth 1:22). The women were returning emptyhanded, but God had a very different future in process. Without any income or source of food, Ruth offered to work in the fields, collecting scraps of barley to sustain them. And according to God's divine orchestration, the field where Ruth worked belonged to none other than Boaz, the previously mentioned son of Rahab and Salmon.

God's fingerprints of providence were all over this meeting. When Ruth told Naomi about her new employer, Naomi saw God's unsurpassed goodness and celebrated: *"He is showing his kindness to us as well as to your dead husband. That man [Boaz] is one of our closest relatives, one of our family redeemers"* (Ruth 2:20, NLT).

The short version for Ruth and Boaz was that a workplace romance blossomed. In following God's path, Boaz purchased the property of Naomi's deceased husband, which more than covered her financial needs. Boaz also brokered a deal to include in the sale the joyous acquisition of Ruth as his wife.

It seemed like the whole township celebrated the marriage. Watch what the town's elders said to Boaz:

> May the Lord make this woman [Ruth] who is coming into your home like Rachel and Leah, from whom all the nation of Israel descended! May you prosper in Ephrathah and be famous in Bethlehem. And may the Lord give you descendants by this young woman who will be like those of our ancestor Perez, the son of Tamar and Judah. (Ruth 4:11–12)

God's blessing knows no bounds. He dots every *i* and crosses every *t* in completing His perfect plan, which was created before time began. Can you see how He weaves the thread of His faithfulness through the seeming mess of these historical realities?

But He wasn't finished yet! Boaz and Ruth conceived a son whom they named Obed—a great name for what new parents crave when raising any newborn: *Oh bed.* Sorry, dad joke alert!

The women of Bethlehem celebrated with Naomi, the one who you will recall renamed herself "bitter." Now the townswomen were singing a new tune over her:

> Praise be to the Lord, who this day has not left you without a guardian-redeemer. May he become famous throughout Israel! He will renew your life and sustain you in your old age. For your daughter-in-law, who loves you and who is better to you than seven sons, has given him birth. (Ruth 4:14–15)

Let's take a moment to praise the Lord! He is amazing and worthy of all honour in executing His plans that transcend our comprehension for the glory of His name.

Praising the Son through the Storm

The book of Ruth concludes by detailing the modified bloodline of God's stunning design, a genealogy which includes some rather familiar names.

> This, then, is the family line of Perez: Perez was the father of Hezron, Hezron the father of Ram, Ram the father of Amminadab, Amminadab the father of Nahshon, Nahshon the father of Salmon, Salmon the father of Boaz, Boaz the father of Obed, Obed the father of Jesse, and Jesse the father of David. (Ruth 4:18–22)

This book's author had a limited frame of reference given their position in time. Today, however, we have the privilege of viewing this genealogy through a much broader lens. We can use it to trace God's threads of grace from the patriarch Abraham right through to Jesus.

This is the account of Jesus's disciple Matthew, the first New Testament author, giving a detailed analysis and cross-referenced validation of the messianic family tree. Watch for the friends we have already met during our journey and note how they play into our shared history in Christ:

> This is the genealogy of *Jesus* the Messiah the son of *David*, the son of *Abraham*: *Abraham* was the father of *Isaac*, *Isaac* the father of *Jacob*, *Jacob* the father of *Judah* and his brothers, *Judah* the father of *Perez* and Zerah, whose mother was *Tamar*, *Perez* the father of Hezron, Hezron the father of Ram, Ram the father of Amminadab, Amminadab the father of Nahshon, Nahshon the father of *Salmon*, *Salmon* the father of

A DIVINE GENEOLOGY

> *Boaz*, whose mother was *Rahab*, *Boaz* the father of *Obed*, whose mother was *Ruth*, *Obed* the father of Jesse, and Jesse the father of King *David*.
>
> *David* was the father of Solomon, whose mother had been Uriah's wife, Solomon the father of Rehoboam, Rehoboam the father of Abijah, Abijah the father of Asa, Asa the father of *Jehoshaphat*, *Jehoshaphat* the father of Jehoram, Jehoram the father of Uzziah, Uzziah the father of Jotham, Jotham the father of Ahaz, Ahaz the father of Hezekiah, Hezekiah the father of Manasseh, Manasseh the father of Amon, Amon the father of Josiah, and Josiah the father of Jeconiah and his brothers at the time of the exile to Babylon.
>
> After the exile to Babylon: Jeconiah was the father of Shealtiel, Shealtiel the father of Zerubbabel, Zerubbabel the father of Abihud, Abihud the father of Eliakim, Eliakim the father of Azor, Azor the father of Zadok, Zadok the father of Akim, Akim the father of Elihud, Elihud the father of Eleazar, Eleazar the father of Matthan, Matthan the father of Jacob, and Jacob the father of *Joseph*, the husband of *Mary*, and *Mary* was the mother of *Jesus* who is called the Messiah.
>
> Thus there were fourteen generations in all from *Abraham* to *David*, fourteen from *David* to the exile to Babylon, and fourteen from the exile to the *Messiah*. (Matthew 1:1–17, emphasis added)

For bonus points, if you're playing along at home, Luke 3:23–38 confirms this history even more extensively and in reverse chronological order. Given Luke's career as a physician, it makes sense that his writings start with Jesus and documents back to the time before Abraham, even past Adam, the first human ever created, to the source of all life: God, who is the Alpha and the Omega, the beginning and the end, who exists outside of time and space and yet made Himself known and saved us through His Son Jesus. Praise God for who He is yesterday, today, and forever!

BACK TO THE FUTURE

The apostle John calls Jesus "the Word" at the beginning of his Holy-Spirit-inspired gospel account. He writes,

> In the beginning was the Word, and the Word was with God, and the Word was God. He was with God in the beginning. Through him all things were made; without him nothing was made that has been made. In him was life, and that life was the light of all mankind. The light shines in the darkness, and the darkness has not overcome it… The Word became flesh and made his dwelling among us. We have seen his glory, the glory of the one and only Son, who came from the Father, full of grace and truth. (John 1:1–5, 14)

This verbiage isn't simply poetic; it's the truth by which all of creation has its being. Everything we see is completely subservient to this truth, either by an active choice today or divine requirement in the future. The person of Jesus is the One whom all of creation praises for its light and life. Philippians 2:9–11 says,

> Now lifted up by God to heaven, a name above all others given, this matchless name possessing. And so, when Jesus' name is called, the knees of everyone should fall, wherever they're residing. Then every tongue in one accord, will say that Jesus the Messiah is Lord, while God the Father praising. (ISV)

According to the Jewish culture, the name of Jesus is interpreted as "Jehovah is Salvation," though Western vernacular often abbreviates His name to "Saviour," both the Saviour of all humanity and our very personal and intimate Lord who cares so deeply about every individual person who has walked, is currently walking, or will one day walk the earth. Jesus's name transcends any limitation known to humanity and all powers above, on, and under the earth. Hope, purpose, history, power, and authority all find their place in and through Him. It doesn't matter who you are or where you have come from, your birth, death, and future have their existence in and through Him.

A mind-blowing detail is that our triune Godhead—the Father, Son and Spirit—stepped into our finite time-space continuum and created a bridge of relationship for anyone who would choose to ask for a reconciled relationship with Jesus, a relationship which our collective sin had severed. Romans 10:13 clearly states that *"everyone who calls on the name of the Lord will be saved"* (ESV). No questions asked. No background checks. No human prejudice. No ifs, ands, or buts! Jesus's life, death and resurrection created the only way for us to be restored in right relationship to God the Father, who loved us enough to send His only Son Jesus to die as a sin substitute for us while we were still dead in ignorance and shame under the crushing weight of sin's eternal consequences.

Praise God that, upon our profession of faith, He adopts us into His family as beloved sons and daughters and heirs of His faithful promise. Our brother Jesus became our Saviour and Lord, and the Holy Spirit gives us His seal of eternal life, empowering us to daily step forward into God's preferred future while praising God for His awe-inspiring and faithful character.

Trillions of people have testified, and millions of books have confirmed, the undeniable reality of our risen Saviour Jesus in a unified chorus of praise that continues to grow louder with each successive generation. From ages past to those yet to discover our sovereign Creator as friend, we stand with Leah, Judah, and all who know Yahweh El Olam, the everlasting Lord, and burst forth in unbridled praise for all that was, is, and is to come. This time we will choose to stand unified and praise the Lord, both now and forever.

Reflection Time

- Christian authors and artists don't write about truths they have mastered but realities they too are continuing to practice. Given this lens for praise, what are the issues you still wrestle with?

- Take a few minutes to read Genesis 32:22–32. As a result of Jacob's physical engagement with God, he thereafter walked with a limp. But this limp/brokenness wasn't a curse; it was a reminder of God's profound impact on him. Are there things in your life that still appear broken? How do you suspect God is using these in developing praise testimonies for His honour and your benefit?

- God may not have restored some broken aspects of your life yesterday or today, and He may not do it tomorrow either. But our praise isn't based on what He does for us. Instead our praise is anchored in what we know God is capable of. We know the truth of His character as our Restorer (Yahweh Elyashib). How can you change your thinking today and praise His character and abilities irrespective of any current adversity?

- Psalm 145:4 says, *"One generation will praise Your works to another, and will declare Your mighty acts"* (NASB). As the biblical genealogy demonstrates, each character encourages us to brag about God's praiseworthy character and deeds to the next generation. This week, choose one or two people to celebrate God's praise with and share the insights you have experienced along your own faith journey.

Conclusion
LAUS DEO

One of my favourite movies is *Apollo 13*. It showcases the indelible qualities of teamwork, courage, perseverance, and tenacity. Besides, what kid didn't want to be an astronaut when they were young? I have my own photo at age ten dressed up as a courageous cosmic explorer in an outfit lovingly crafted by my mum. Thanks so much, Mum! Awesome job.

While the movie depicts how a tiny flaw in a manufactured component led to the near-catastrophic deaths of three astronauts during a 1970s moon mission, I'm continually inspired by Gene Kranz's perspective as NASA's flight director. As the odds stacked up against this intrepid crew, labouring tirelessly far beyond the earth's atmosphere, the mission control director spoke words to his earthbound team that many in his shoes may have been too scared to verbalize: "This could be the worst disaster NASA's ever experienced." Everyone could hear his foreboding tone. Yet from this ominous pessimism, Kranz, played by Ed Harris, respectfully challenged that likely outcome: "With all due respect, sir, I believe this is gonna be our finest hour."[30]

This wasn't just a nice phrase to bolster the mood in the room. It emanated from Kranz's uncompromising personal belief and catalyzed a renewed hope among the scores of directors and technicians diligently labouring at mission control to bring these men safely back to earth.

Leah did something similar with her intentional choice to praise the Lord. This matriarch of the faith lived in an unhappy household under very challenging circumstances, yet she committed to praising her Lord. She chose to thoughtfully consider the Lord's historical goodness, provision, and answers and spoke to her own soul in a similar way to how David did: *"Why am I discouraged? Why is my heart so sad? I will put my hope in God! I will praise him—my Savior and my God!"* (Psalm 42:5–6, NLT) With this powerful declaration and personal action, she offered a universal invitation to anyone who has ears to hear.

Praise marks a deliberate determination to rehearse God's character and promises irrespective of our own challenges. For some sceptics, praising God in every circumstance will make absolutely no sense, especially not in the darkest nights of the soul, yet this is what we, as Jesus's disciples, are called to do along our spiritual journey.

The purpose of praise assists in changing our situationally informed perspective towards the One from whom all heaven and earth derives their being and ascribes greatness to our sovereign God of the universe, and to His Son, King Jesus, who reigns on heaven's throne above every power and authority from eternity past to eternity future through the vehicle of the Holy Spirit. In short, heartfelt praise honours our Creator while transforming us in the process.

The choice to praise is a daily commitment to celebrate the character and reality of our Creator God and Saviour Jesus by accessing the transformational power of the Holy Spirit. Depending on the season, praise may look like a fleeting God-inspired thought, a verse, a lyric, tears of lament, a curious question, an arm raised in surrender, silent contemplation, or a shout because you believe His goodness is bigger

---

[30] *Apollo 13,* directed by Ron Howard (Los Angeles, CA: Universal Pictures, 1995).

than what you can see right now. There could be a multitude of other expressions. Ultimately, it's not the method that is key but the One to whom our hearts are directing this praise, as He alone operates as the pinnacle of power and authority.

If this hasn't been your regular personal practice to date, you may feel disqualified from even participating. Or maybe you've tried and been crushed by the heavy burden of seeming abandonment. My friend, I stand with you in these past thoughts and experiences. Yet I also encourage you. These feelings can be fickle and fluid. Our faith is called to testify to the truth of who we know our God to be. So stand to your feet, know the forgiveness of a Saviour who doesn't hold anything against you, and start again, even if it's with a tiny whisper of acknowledgement.

Zechariah 4:10 reads, *"Do not despise these small beginnings, for the Lord rejoices to see the work begin, to see the plumb line in Zerubbabel's hand"* (NLT). Whether praising and thanking God for the smallest glimpses of His faithfulness or exuberantly shouting in joyous recognition of God's abundant grace, God loves to see our recognition of who He is and what He has done. Just as every godly blessing is ultimately a forest of abundance in disguise, so the Lord implores us not to underestimate the humble beginnings of actioning this celebration with praise-filled faith, given all He has promised and will fulfill.

If the name Zerubbabel happens to look familiar, it may be because you just read it in Matthew's genealogy. Zerubbabel was the governor of the province of Judah and he worked alongside Nehemiah in supervising the reconstruction of Jerusalem's temple of praise. As another of our biblical mentors, he shines a light towards the coming Christ who would be divinely incarnated through Mary ten generations later.

In some seasons, praise requires more intentionality. But each time we engage in our calling, we renew our minds, hearts, and will in perceiving God's faithful character and sovereign power with increasing clarity.

Like Leah, the invitation to holistic surrender is just the beginning; the journey is far more fulfilling than our finite minds can comprehend.

No one can fully describe or appreciate the beautiful exchange that occurs when we choose to praise. In the busyness of life, we can create an environment that draws us close to His heart. This act of focused reverence and humble obedience makes room in our lives for His greatness. It opens our eyes wider, and our hearts deeper, to hear the Holy Spirit's gentle voice. It fills our spirits with the hope-filled revelation that forever finds its purpose in Christ.

THE PINNACLE OF PRAISE

A friend and colleague recently gave me a hand-painted rock with the phrase *Laus Deo* written on it. Translated from Latin, this means "Praise be to God." It is a beautiful art piece, but I was immensely curious to investigate the story behind the phrase and discovered that these words are also engraved on the east face of the aluminum capping atop the Washington Monument in Washington DC.

Standing 555 feet tall, this colossal white granite and marble obelisk was designed by architect Robert Mills. Construction was completed on December 6, 1884 to honour George Washington as America's first president. While this icon showcases America's modern-day ingenuity, the memorial was also designed to honour the eternal founding Father of the nation. As the pledge of allegiance reminds us, America is "one nation under God."

Following its completion, the Height of Buildings Act was passed by the sixty-first United States Congress in 1910, effectively preventing the building of any structure in Washington exceeding the height of the monument. As a result, this holy declaration at the obelisk's peak stands uncontested upon the highest point of arguably the world's most powerful city.[31] Many other skyscrapers have since been erected in neighbouring cities and stand with boastful pride above this sacred message.[32]

Until the world we inhabit is no more, the enemy will try to overshadow our praise of God with his own lies and humanity's pride. But

---

[31] "Washington Monument," *National Park Service*. Date of access: July 30, 2025 (https://www.nps.gov/wamo/learn/historyculture/index.htm); "Washington Monument," *National Park Foundation*. Date of access: July 30, 2025 (https://www.nationalparks.org/explore/parks/washington-monument).

[32] "Tallest Buildings," *Skyscraper Center*. Date of access: July 30, 2025 (https://www.skyscrapercenter.com/buildings?status=completed&material=all&function=all&location=country-united-states&year=2023).

nothing will ever compare to the surpassing praise for the greatness of our God. As Psalm 145:3 asserts, *"Great is the Lord and most worthy of praise; his greatness no one can fathom."*

A Call to Action

Every Christ-follower has been given a measure of influence and has the express purpose of making godly changes in their sphere of connection. We are called to showcase the goodness of God in every circumstance of life through praise, worship, and thanksgiving and to invite others into this same transformational relationship with our Saviour and Lord Jesus Christ. As Hebrews 13:15–16 says,

> Therefore, let us offer through Jesus a continual sacrifice of praise to God, proclaiming our allegiance to his name. And don't forget to do good and to share with those in need. These are the sacrifices that please God. (NLT)

There are gifts and talents we have been given to serve in this high calling. We can use them to great effect, but each one is to be grounded on the bedrock of praise since an intimate relationship with God is our purpose and testimony.

This sacrifice of praise is purely directed toward the person of Jesus and should never be adulterated by any human claims of ownership.

The apostle John offered a divine insight for his own purpose in this matter: *"It is the bridegroom [Jesus] who marries the bride [His church], and the bridegroom's friend [His followers] is simply glad to stand with him and hear his vows. Therefore, I am filled with joy at his success"* (John 3:29, NLT). John was asserting that he didn't want or deserve any special recognition or praise directed back to himself. He was simply ecstatic to watch Jesus transform the lives of all those around him, and to humbly act as a conduit to this divine change.

Later in Revelation, John continued, with Holy Spirit inspiration, to narrate the end of the age. He saw a war break out in heaven. Every power that didn't submit to the name of Jesus was vanquished forever. Today we celebrate with John, who victoriously stated,

> The salvation and the power and the kingdom of our God, and the ruling authority of his Christ, have now come, because the accuser of our brothers and sisters, the one who accuses them day and night before our God, has been thrown down. But they overcame him by the blood of the Lamb and by the word of their testimony, and they did not love their lives so much that they were afraid to die. Therefore you heavens rejoice, and all who reside in them! (Revelation 12:10–12, NET)

What an incredible ending! The Lion of Judah has conquered every power and authority and Christ's disciples now stand with Him in victory because His blood, as the Lamb of God, was poured out for all in loving surrender together with the powerful words of our divine testimony of praise.

Allow this to sink in. Christ is celebrated as heaven's champion and His followers are honoured for using praise in their life-giving testimony to point people towards the Lion of Judah.

Let us never allow this powerful weapon of praise to fall silent. For as long as we have breath, for as long as we have strength, until the end of time and beyond, we join with the hosts of heaven, saints past and present, and all of creation in glorifying the Lord from whom all things forever have their being.

With all that we are and everything we have, let us perpetually utilize the divine weapon of God-centred praise to break down strongholds, overcome compliancy, and transcend the reality we see around us for the glory and honour of our triune Godhead, whom we are forever privileged to call Abba Father and the Lion of Judah.

In conclusion, the writer of the final psalm composes the greatest "Hallelujah" he can muster given human limitations. He not only calls on everyone and everything to join in this exuberant eternal chorus with angels and saints alike but outlines the who, where, why, and how of praise.

Talk about leaving it all out on the court! He calls for all of creation to join in the most majestic anthem ever composed. It will never cease to resonate throughout eternity.

In this moment, we stand together with Leah and Judah, with Adam, Abraham, the entire messianic lineage, and everyone since adopted into His family. Let us raise our voices with people from all generations, nationalities, cultures, colours, and demographics, including those past, present, and yet to come. Let's create a sound of praise that transcends time and space, which silences the enemy and brings ceaseless honour to the Father, Son, and Holy Spirit in passionately testifying that this time we will praise the Lord forever and ever, amen.

> Hallelujah! Praise God in his holy house of worship, praise him under the open skies; praise him for his acts of power, praise him for his magnificent greatness; praise with a blast on the trumpet, praise by strumming soft strings; praise him with castanets and dance, praise him with banjo and flute; praise him with cymbals and a big bass drum, praise him with fiddles and mandolin. Let every living, breathing creature praise God! Hallelujah! (Psalm 150:1–6 MSG)

Reflection Time

- As a fitting celebration, I would strongly encourage you to praise God while watching the Elevation Worship song entitled "Praise". This passionate and truth-filled declaration of Psalm 150 is set to music in honouring our Maker, Redeemer and Counsellor.[33]

---

[33] "Praise (feat. Brandon Lake, Chris Brown & Chandler Moore) | Elevation Music," *YouTube*. Date of access: August 5, 2025 (https://www.youtube.com/watch?v=f2oxGYpuLkw&list=RDf2oxGYpuLkw&start_radio=1&ab_channel=ElevationWorship).

ABOUT THE AUTHOR

What a blessing it was to be born in Australia to godly parents who exampled praise for our family as we followed Dad's professional career around New South Wales and into the diverse social, cultural, and religious setting of Indonesia. My professional career led me from radiation therapist, to registered clinical counsellor, to pastor, to army chaplain, and most recently to company chaplain for a manufacturing company in North America (Lynden Door Inc./Alliance Door Products Canada). I have been blessed to be married to my awesome wife Kristy for more than two decades, with whom we have two amazing adult kids. With qualifications in radiation therapy, counselling, ministerial leadership, theology, and lived experience in several countries, I humbly present this accumulated wisdom in service of the One to whom all praise is due.

BIBLIOGRAPHY

Abrahams, Lynn, *Unleashing Courageous Faith*. (Croydon, AU: Green Hill Publishing, 2022).

Angelou, Maya, *Rainbow in the Cloud: The Wisdom and Spirit of Maya Angelou* (New York, NY: Random House, 2014).

Apollo 13, directed by Ron Howard (Los Angeles, CA: Universal Pictures, 1995).

Barrier, Dr. Roger, "8 Hebrew Words for 'Praise' Every Christian Needs to Know, *Crosswalk*. April 26, 2021 (www.crosswalk.com/faith/spiritual-life/8-hebrew-words-for-praise-every-christian-needs-to-know.html).

Bonhoeffer, Dietrich, *God Is in the Manger: Reflections on Advent and Christmas* (Louisville, KY: Westminster John Knox Press, 2010).

Bowlby, John, *Attachment and Loss, Volume Three* (New York, NY: Basic Books, 1982).

Breland, Jeremy, "Abram to Abraham? Why Did He Do It?" *Walterboro Live*. June 28, 2020, (walterborolive.com/stories/abram-to-abraham-why-did-he-do-it-faith,32425).

Cloud, Dr. Henry, *Boundaries for Leaders: Results, Relationships, and Being Ridiculously in Charge* (New York, NY: Harper Business, 2013).

Covey, Stephen R., *The 7 Habits of Highly Effective People: Powerful Lessons in Personal Change* (New York, NY: Free Press, 2004).

Groeschel, Craig, *Hope in the Dark* (Grand Rapids, MI: Zondervan, 2018).

Harris, Russ, *The Happiness Trap* (Boulder, CO: Shambhala Publications, 2008).

Harvard Health, "Benefits of Mindfulness," *Help Guide*. Aug 30 2024 (www.helpguide.org/harvard/benefits-of-mindfulness.htm).

Hodges, Chris, *Out of the Cave* (Nashville, TN: Nelson Books, 2021).

Houston, Brian, *Live Love Lead* (Sydney, NSW: HarperCollins Publishers, 2015).

Lewis, C.S., *The Problem of Pain* (San Francisco, CA: HarperOne, 2018).

Liebscher, Banning, *Rooted: The Hidden Places Where God Develops You* (Colorado Springs, CO: Waterbrook Press, 2019).

Mohler, Albert, *Conviction to Lead: 25 Principles for Leadership That Matters* (Ada, MI: Baker Publishing Group, 2014).

"Saints Among Us: The Work of Mother Teresa," *Time*. December 29, 1975 (https://time.com/archive/6878542/saints-among-us-the-work-of-mother-teresa).

Nepstad, Shaun, *Don't Quit in the Dip* (Franklin, TN: Worthy Books, 2023).

Peterson, Eugene H. *Follow the Leader*. Regent College, Vancouver, Audio CD, 2000.

Ritchie, Daniel, "God Shouts to Us in Our Pain," *Desiring God*. January 17, 2016 (www.desiringgod.org/articles/god-shouts-to-us-in-our-pain).

Rohn, Jim, "Being Successful Is a Personal Choice," *Jim Rohn*. Date of access: July 29, 2025 (https://www.jimrohn.com/success-is-a-personal-choice).

Scazzero, Peter, *Emotionally Healthy Spirituality Day by Day* (Grand Rapids, MI: Zondervan, 2014).

Story, Laura, *When God Doesn't Fix It: Lessons You Never Wanted To Learn, Truths You Can't Live Without* (Nashville, TN: W Publishing Group, 2015).

"The Serenity Prayer: Original Version, Author, and Bible Truths," *Crosswalk*. November 19, 2023 (www.crosswalk.com/faith/prayer/serenity-prayer-applying-3-truths-from-the-bible.html).

Wallin, David J., *Attachment in Psychotherapy* (New York, NY: Guilford Press, 2007).

Warnock, Adrian, "God Breaks Those He Wants to Make Great," *Patheos*. October 18 2009, (www.patheos.com/blogs/adrianwarnock/2009/10/god-breaks-those-he-wants-to-make-great).

Warren, Rick, *The Purpose Driven Life*. Grand Rapids, Michigan, Zondervan, 2002.

Wiggins, Jonathan, *Walking with Lions* (Birmingham, AL: Association of Related Churches, 2021).

Yancey, Philip, *Disappointment with God: Three Questions No One Asks Aloud* (Grand Rapids, MI: Zondervan, 1997).

www.ingramcontent.com/pod-product-compliance
Lightning Source LLC
LaVergne TN
LVHW041253080426
835510LV00009B/723